A PECULIAR PARADISE

A Peculiar Paradise

A HISTORY OF BLACKS IN OREGON, 1788–1940

SECOND EDITION

Elizabeth McLagan

Oregon State University Press Corvallis
Published in cooperation with Oregon Black Pioneers

Library of Congress Cataloging-in-Publication Data

Names: McLagan, Elizabeth, 1947- author. | Oregon Black Pioneers.
Title: A peculiar paradise : a history of blacks in Oregon, 1788–1940 / Elizabeth McLagan.
Description: Second edition. | Corvallis : Oregon State University Press, 2022. | "Published in cooperation with Oregon Black Pioneers." | Includes bibliographical references and index.
Identifiers: LCCN 2022037305 | ISBN 9780870712210 (trade paperback) | ISBN 9780870714023 (ebook)
Subjects: LCSH: African Americans—Oregon—History. | Oregon—History. | Oregon—Race relations.
Classification: LCC E185.93.O7 M3 2022 | DDC 305.8960730795—dc23/eng/20220816
LC record available at https://lccn.loc.gov/2022037305

∞ This paper meets the requirements of ANSI/NISO Z39.48-1992 (Permanence of Paper).

Originally published in 1980 by the Georgian Press.
Second edition published in 2022 by Oregon State University Press.
Printed in the United States of America

Published in cooperation with Oregon Black Pioneers.

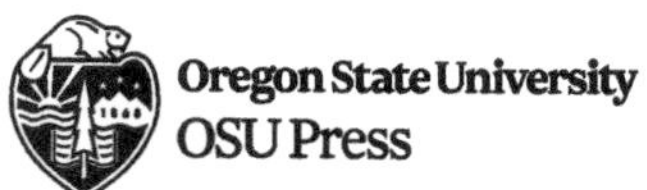

Oregon State University Press
121 The Valley Library
Corvallis OR 97331-4501
541-737-3166 • fax 541-737-3170
www.osupress.oregonstate.edu

For Marie Smith and Otto Rutherford

Contents

Foreword

I first read *A Peculiar Paradise* in the early 2000s after I was recruited to serve on the board of Oregon Northwest Black Pioneers (later renamed Oregon Black Pioneers) by Willie Richardson. I was eager to learn all I could about Oregon's Black history, and I had heard that *A Peculiar Paradise* was the only book of its kind on the topic. Sadly, I found that it was out of print, but I was able to secure a few copies online and at a used bookstore. It became, for me, a collector's item.

Growing up in California, my knowledge of Oregon history in general was pretty much limited to hearing about the Lewis and Clark Expedition, and that the expedition included a Black slave. Like many others, I had assumed that the earliest Blacks in Oregon had come with the workers on the Transcontinental Railroad in the late 1800s and then with workers in the Portland shipyards in the 1940s. While the largest influx of Blacks did take place during those times, I would soon read about the lives of those who came to Oregon far earlier and the conditions in which they carved out lives for themselves.

A few years later, Willie and I began to explore the idea of Oregon Northwest Black Pioneers producing its own book on Oregon's Black history. Initially we had planned to produce an updated version of *A Peculiar Paradise*, extending the date range and expanding the scope to all locations in Oregon. I was able to meet with the author, Elizabeth McLagan, in Portland to discuss our plans and to hear about her work in developing the book. She was overjoyed that our organization had made a commitment to continue this work.

I discussed with her how she came to write this landmark book, originally published in 1980. *A Peculiar Paradise* was the result of a project begun in 1977 that later evolved into the Oregon Black History Project, a project of the Comprehensive Employment and Training Act (CETA). An Oregon Black History Project Task Force was formed, headed by staff at the Oregon Historical Society and including an array of educators, historians, and community members from the public and private sectors. McLagan was hired to direct the project, and she ended up writing *A Peculiar Paradise.* She compiled sources from earlier projects and publications, including manuscripts, oral interviews, and photographs, and then carefully reviewed them to write a narrative of Oregon's Black history up to 1940.

McLagan's dream was that someone would take up the mantle and continue this work. In the preface to her book, she stated, "Because of circumstances of limited funds and time, the history of rural black people in this century is missing. A second volume covering the period after 1940 is necessary. This book is but a beginning." But thirty years later, there had not been much progress. Few scholarly works had been published on rural Black history or Black history post-1940 that could be a companion to McLagan's book.

Oregon Black Pioneers was inspired and honored to take on this task, but ultimately we decided to take a regional approach to publications instead. We first looked exclusively at Marion and Polk counties. Marion County was the home county of our organization, and we had already developed relationships with local historians and historical organizations that were more than willing to help with research and expertise. In 2011 we self-published *Perseverance: A History of African Americans in Oregon's Marion and Polk Counties*. The book was the culmination of the research initiated in 1993 by Willie Richardson and other members of the Oregon Northwest Black Pioneers Board.

As the years went by, word spread about our book and the findings from our research. Willie and I started giving presentations to historical and civic organizations, schools, and even governmental agencies. We found that the public was amazed by the largely untold stories of Oregon's Black history and was hungry to learn more. Wherever we went, we were encouraged to continue this work and to make it available to the public and particularly to schools.

Our presentations captured the imagination of local communities, whose museums became our research partners in exploring Black history statewide. Collaborations began to spring up, beginning with tabletop displays at community events, including a map showing the presence of Blacks all over the state, county by county. It became a visual magnet at events, as it introduced Oregonians to history they had not known before.

The foundational pieces of that map began with information and pictures contained in *A Peculiar Paradise*.

Our small displays then evolved into exhibits hosted around the state at museums like the Oregon Historical Society Museum in Portland and the Museum of Natural and Cultural History at the University of Oregon in Eugene. Many of these exhibits covered more recent history, challenging Oregon Black Pioneers to conduct original research on Black history after World War II. In this way, we were meeting the need for contemporary research that Elizabeth McLagan had pointed out so many years ago.

What is most intriguing to me about Oregon's Black history is that in spite of exclusionary laws, ongoing discrimination, and a small Black population, families survived and thrived here in both urban and rural communities. Where there were greater numbers, Black communities with businesses, churches, and schools were established and flourished.

Over the years, *A Peculiar Paradise* has become a vital resource for research being done on Black history in Oregon. The book has been cited many times and has inspired other authors to look deeper into Oregon's Black history and publish their findings. Perhaps the greatest outcome of the collective work that *A Peculiar Paradise* began is that the information the work has revealed is now being incorporated into school curricula at all levels. Every year, more Oregonians are being introduced to this hidden part of Oregon's history.

Original copies of *A Peculiar Paradise* are even harder to find today. It is my prayer that republishing this book will make this important history more accessible, inspiring new generations to pursue the author's original intent—to research and document Oregon's Black history.

Gwen Carr
Emeritus Board Member
Oregon Black Pioneers

Note on the Second Edition

Since the original publication of *A Peculiar Paradise* in 1980, historians have uncovered new information about many of the individuals and stories featured in this book. Oregon Black Pioneers has referenced this information in the second edition of the book through the insertion of brief footnotes. These are intended to provide additional context and direction for further research. Where appropriate, these footnotes also serve to correct inaccuracies in the first edition.

The author occasionally uses antiquated racial terminology that today's readers may find offensive. However, with the exception of corrections to minor spelling and stylistic errors, the original text has been preserved exactly as written in order to maintain the historical integrity of this important work.

Preface

My involvement with the Oregon Black History Project began in December 1977, when I was hired to direct a year-long research project that would culminate in a manuscript covering the history of the black people of Oregon to the beginning of World War II. This project was funded by a grant from the Comprehensive Employment and Training Act. We inherited a number of oral history tapes and photographs from a previous phase of the project, funded by a grant from the Bicentennial Commission.

It quickly became evident that the history of a small minority had to be placed in the larger context of the history of the attitudes of the white community of Oregon in an attempt to uncover, if not fully explain, the peculiar and persistent prejudice against black people that existed in Oregon. Because of the nature of much of the material concerning the lives of individual blacks, especially in the nineteenth century when family records are meager and public attention was turned away from the small black community, much of the information is episodic.

The first chapter considers the role of black people in the settlement of Oregon from the appearance of Marcus Lopez in 1788 to 1850. The next four chapters describe the attitudes toward blacks and other minorities evident in exclusion laws, the slavery controversy, and various anti-black legislation considered and passed between 1843 and 1875. The next two chapters deal with the experience of rural black people in the nineteenth century, and the founding and development of the black community of Portland from 1850 to 1940. A chapter is then devoted to a description of the kinds of prejudice black people faced in Oregon, followed by a chapter dealing with attempts to pass civil rights legislation and to repeal existing anti-black legislation, including a brief comparison of anti-black legislation and attitudes in the neighboring states of California and Washington. The final chapter is an epilogue briefly describing the period after 1940.

The ambiguities inherent in writing a history of a minority with which the author cannot personally identify are not, in this case, unfelt or unaccounted for. I would not weigh the difficulties of being a woman in a male dominated society as equal with the difficulties of being a member of a minority. But if the intensity of the experience of discrimination is not comparable, the fact of it is. I have tried to resist general definitions of either the black community or the white community and to allow, wherever possible, the past to speak for itself. The oral history interviews that were collected, that I listened to over and over, were a major source of information and inspiration, and taught me what I could never experience. I have had spiritual mentors in two black people in particular, to whom this book is dedicated.

Because of the circumstances of limited funds and time, the history of rural black people in this century is missing. A second volume covering the period after 1940 is necessary. This book is but a beginning.

I would like to express my personal thanks to my research assistants David Wood, Patricia Passmore, and particularly to Martha Anderson, one of those who voiced the original idea for such a project. Margaret Sherman and Linda Freed shared in the painstaking task of transcribing the oral history tapes and typed some of the early manuscript drafts.

To the members of the Board of Directors of the project goes the credit for obtaining the original funds to support the research and much of the writing of the manuscript. They provided continued support and encouragement. Further, the members of the editorial committee spent long hours reading successive manuscript drafts, and their suggestions and comments were invaluable. All or portions of the manuscript were also read by Darrell Wax and Thomas McClintock, members of the faculty of the history department at Oregon State University. Their contributions and encouragement are gratefully acknowledged. A special thanks is due to Helen Warbington, whose tireless work behind the scenes was much appreciated. I would also like to thank Kim MacColl, who agreed to publish the book.

The staffs of the Oregon Historical Society, the Multnomah County Library, the Oregon State Library and Oregon State Archives provided generous assistance to the members of the research staff. For the entire project, I wish to thank the people who believed enough in the book to order advance copies. Your patience and support are much appreciated.

Finally, I would like to express my thanks to William Beeson, for his personal support and encouragement, and to my mother, Betty McLagan, whose generous assistance has helped to make the timely publication of this book a reality.

Elizabeth McLagan
October 1980

1

Into the Wilderness

Blacks in Oregon 1788–1850

On December 21, 1787, the *Lady Washington* set sail from the Cape Verde Islands, heading south and west toward Cape Horn and into the Pacific Ocean, then turning north to explore the coast of the North American continent. Among those on board was Marcus Lopez, the first black person to set foot on Oregon soil.[a] The voyage of the *Lady Washington* originated in Boston, Massachusetts, sponsored by businessmen who were interested in the potential sea otter trade with the Northwest Coast Indians. Captained by Robert Gray, the vessel stopped at the Cape Verde Islands, located off the west coast of Africa, to replenish supplies. Marcus Lopez, a native of those islands, joined the voyage, hired as a cabin boy by Robert Gray. Robert Haswell, the nineteen-year-old first mate who kept a diary of the voyage, observed that the Cape Verde Islands were blessed with an abundance of tropical fruit, and the black people were "as contented a people as I ever saw, polite and hospitable."[1]

The Northwest Coast must have seemed a strange and fearful place to Lopez, who was accustomed to tropical surroundings. Haswell's first observations of the coast of Oregon mentioned a "delightful country thickly inhabited and clothed with woods and verdue with many charming streams of water gushing from the valleys." He compared the numbers of birds they saw to a "hive with the bees swarming." Passing close to the shoreline near the Alsea River, he noted the large number of Indians, who "appeared to be a very hostile and warlike people."[2]

On August 14, 1788, the ship entered a bay near the present town of

a Historian Melissa Darby claims four Afro-Latinos reached Oregon as early as 1579 aboard English privateer Sir Francis Drake's ship *Golden Hinde*. See Melissa Darby, *Thunder Go North: The Hunt for Francis Drake's Fair and Good Bay*, chapter 5 (Salt Lake City: University of Utah Press, 2017). Free and enslaved Blacks were also common aboard Spanish ships in the Pacific throughout the 1600s, and Tillamook and Nehalem oral traditions suggest Blacks may have washed ashore as shipwreck survivors.

Tillamook,[b] Oregon, casting anchor to take on food and water for the crew and animals on board ship, tasks that were assigned to Marcus Lopez.

The first contact with the Indians was friendly. They visited the ship, bringing presents of berries and boiled crabs, a welcome change of diet for many of the crew who were suffering from scurvy. The Indians also handed otter skins on board the ship, satisfied with the knives and axes given in return. When crew members went ashore to gather wood and food for the animals, the Indians brought them fruit to eat, but were armed and watchful.

> The natives while we were at work on shore behaved themselves with great propriety, frequently bringing us fruit, but they always kept themselves armed, and never ventured nigh us but with their knives in their hands ready to strike.[3]

August 16th began peacefully. Indians again visited the ship and traded crabs, dried salmon and berries for buttons and other novelties. That afternoon, with little to do but wait for the next day's tide, the crew went ashore again. The Indians had behaved in a friendly manner, and the white men were not well armed. They visited the village, were offered food, and entertained by demonstrations of agility with arrows and spears. A war dance climaxed the entertainment, then the crew strolled back down the beach to search for clams.

Marcus Lopez, busy cutting grass for the livestock, stuck his cutlass in the sand while carrying a load of grass to a boat. One of the Indians saw his opportunity and took the cutlass. Another member of the crew observed the theft and called out, threatening to shoot, hoping that the Indian would drop the cutlass and flee. Marcus was warned not to interfere with the Indians, but he chased the man who had taken his cutlass into the village. Other members of the crew followed Lopez, offering a reward if he were returned unharmed. The chief refused to intercede, and suggested that the crew members rescue Lopez themselves. They found him surrounded by a group of well armed Indians, who saw the men approaching, killed Lopez, and attacked the crew members, who had to run for their lives. Haswell made one final observation of the event that ended the life of Marcus Lopez.

> We knew little of the manners and customs of the people, our stay among them was so short . . . It was folly for us to have gone ashore so ill armed but it proved sufficient warning to us to be well armed ever afterwards . . .[4]

Sixteen years later, a black slave called York reached the mouth of the

b Garibaldi, Oregon

Columbia River near modern Astoria. He was a member of the Lewis and Clark Expedition, the first federally funded overland journey to the Pacific Coast and back. Thomas Jefferson, who had favored an expedition to the Pacific Coast for over twenty years, was able to purchase France's holdings on the North American continent in 1803. The sale of Louisiana Territory was prompted by a black revolt on an island in the Caribbean that unseated the French government from power. France was engaged in a fight to retain control of the island known as Santo Domingo, a valuable sugar producing area with a large black population. Fearing that Napoleon intended to restore slavery, an army of black men was organized and eventually defeated the French troops, establishing the independent nation of Haiti. Napoleon was short of funds and feared the loss of Santo Domingo, his stepping stone to the North American continent. He sold the Louisiana Territory, withdrawing to Europe. The United States bought the area for a bargain price, and the stage was set for expansion to the Pacific Coast.

President Jefferson sent Meriwether Lewis and William Clark west with specific instructions. They were to find a water route from the Missouri to the Pacific Ocean if one existed, to record the geographic features, climate, wildlife, vegetation; to establish contact with the Indian tribes and gather general information about the region. The expedition, if successful, was certain to strengthen American claims to the vast area between the western boundary of Louisiana Territory and the Pacific Ocean.

York was the slave of William Clark, and was born at his master's home in Virginia. He was a man of impressive size: six feet two inches tall, of large build with jet black skin and thick curly hair.[c] He was a skilled hunter, and had some knowledge of French, which proved essential in translating for the guide Charbonneau, who spoke no English.[d] He was adept in living off the land as Clark observed in his diary: "My man York killed a buffalo bull, as he informed me for his tongue and marrow bones."[5] On more than one occasion the journals of the expedition recorded that York was a great curiosity to the Indian tribes who visited the camp to see him and supplied the party with provisions.

---

c Such physical descriptions of York are speculative. No images were made of York during his lifetime, and his height and appearance are not recorded in any primary source in such exact terms. William Clark describes York's appearance only generally in the expedition journals, calling him "fat" on August 24, 1804, and "large" on January 1, 1805.

d York did not speak French. This myth comes from the writing of a Canadian fur trader at Fort Mandan named Charles McKenzie, who saw Charbonneau speaking to "a mulatto who spoke bad French and worse English." Later authors assumed this "mulatto" was York; however, McKenzie's "mulatto" was more likely Pierre Cruzatte, Francois Labiche, or George Drouillard—all mixed-race French/Indigenous members of the Corps of Discovery. See Darrell Millner, "York of the Corps of Discovery," *Oregon Historical Quarterly* 104, no. 3 (2003).

> Some of the party had also told the Indians that we had a man with us who was black and had short curling hair, this had excited their curiosity very much, and they seemed quite as anxious to see this monster as they were the merchandise which we had to barter for their horses.[6]

York enjoyed this attention and was fond of displaying his great physical strength. He boasted that he had once been a wild animal, but was tamed by his master. The Indians called him "great medicine."

Although a slave, York enjoyed a measure of equality during the expedition. He was permitted to vote with the rest of the members of the party on the site of the winter camp, located on the south side of the Columbia River three miles up a small creek, where elk were plentiful. Here they constructed a small fort, named for the friendly Clatsop Indians who lived nearby, and spent the cold, monotonous winter tanning elk hides for clothing, making salt, and finding what diversions they could from the endless rain and tedious diet.

York remained with Captain Clark after the expedition returned to St. Louis in September 1806, where they were hailed as heroes. In 1811, he was given his freedom[e] and a six horse team and wagon, while the enlisted men of the expedition received 320 acres of land and double pay.

The Lewis and Clark Expedition was the highlight of York's life, and a great adventure. He was an instant success with the Indian tribes. Indian children would follow him, darting away if he turned toward them. The women found him attractive and quarreled over him. Warriors respected him and even suggested that he overthrow Clark, subdue the soldiers and become their chief.[f] One Flathead Chief, convinced that York had painted his face black as a sign of war, was only placated when York uncovered his head to reveal his short, wooly hair. Later, York was fond of repeating stories about the expedition, and "as the drams went down the extravagance of the stories went up, with an outcome marvelous indeed."[7]

Various stories survive concerning York's later life. According to one account, after he received his freedom he ran a freight service between Richmond and Nashville. This business failed, and he became a free servant, was abused, and regretted leaving the security of the Clark home.[g] In 1832,

---

e Letters from William Clark to his brother Jonathan discovered in Louisville in the late 1980s revealed that York was still enslaved at least until 1811, and perhaps as late as November 1815 when he was working for John Hite Clark in Kentucky. See Millner, and James Holmberg, ed., *Dear Brother: Letters of William Clark to Jonathan Clark* (2002).

f This unsourced claim is questionable.

g The source of this suspicious claim is none other than William Clark, who reported it to author Washington Irving in 1832. Irving wrote that York cried, "Damn this freedom. I have never had a happy day since I got it," before heading to rejoin Clark. How Clark would have learned of this he was on his way back to the Clark family and died of cholera in Tennessee. In the same year, a trapper named Zenas Leonard claimed to have met a black man living as a chief among the Crow Indians. This man told the trapper that he had first visited the Crow country with Lewis and Clark and had returned later to settle among the Indians, taking four women as wives. When this chief met the trapper, he claimed he had been living among the Indians for ten years. If this story is true, then this black chief was none other than York. A final clue to York's fate is a theory that he was found frozen to death on a road in Albemarle County, Virginia, at the age of ninety.[8]

York's story ends in mystery but, although he was forgotten by historians, he was remembered in Northwest Indian legends.[h] Jesse Applegate preserved a story he heard from Indians near The Dalles as he and his family, just arrived in Oregon, were rafting down the Columbia River. Indians passing in canoes asked the settlers for tobacco:

> The spokesman was a large stout man with more black in his skin than a red man. His eyes were not really black, but looked at our distance like burnt holes in a blanket. He was bare headed, I do not mean bald headed, but that he wore no unnatural covering on his head. He surely did not need to, for this son of an African sire, and a native daughter of the Walla Walla, Cayuse, Klickitat, Chemomichat, Spokane or Wasco-pum tribe, had an immense shock of grizzly, almost curly hair, which grew down to his ears and to within an inch of his nose, making his head seem unnaturally large. Some of our party gave them a little tobacco and they passed on. Now, who was this shock-headed heathen? They said he was the son of a negro man who came to the coast with Lewis and Clark's expedition as cook, about forty years before the time of which I am speaking, and who . . . because of his black skin, wooly head, large proportions, thick lips . . . was so petted by the squaws that he left the expedition in the Walla Walla country and remained with the native daughters.[9]

The early maritime voyages to the Pacific Coast and the Lewis and Clark Expedition proved to be of enormous value to American interests in the Pacific Northwest. The abundance of sea otter prompted other U.S. maritime voyages, until by the turn of the century Americans dominated the sea otter trade. The Lewis and Clark Expedition found a great potential for fur trading, not only in the relatively inaccessible Pacific Northwest but further east in

---

exclamation by York is unclear, as Clark was in Missouri when York allegedly said it in Kentucky. Historians have expressed serious doubts on the authenticity of this claim.

h More accurately, remembered in white men's accounts of Indian legends. There is no truth to Applegate's story about York leaving the expedition to remain in the Oregon Country.

the region from the Mississippi Valley to the Rocky Mountains. The journals of the expedition also praised the agricultural potential of the Willamette Valley. These were published and widely read, and prompted many settlers to come to the area.

In the first forty years of the nineteenth century, it was again to be the American fur trappers and traders, operating briefly in the Pacific Northwest and widely in the Rocky Mountains, who would open the great overland immigrant routes which brought the settlers west to Oregon. The fur trade in Oregon was dominated by the Hudson's Bay Company, operating as a private monopoly supported by the British government. Headed by Chief Factor John McLoughlin and located at Fort Vancouver, the company exercised nearly total control over fur trade in Oregon from 1821 into the 1840s.

An American attempt to compete with the British was launched in 1810, when John J. Astor organized the Pacific Fur Company and sent two expeditions to establish a trading post at the mouth of the Columbia River near modern Astoria. One of the expeditions traveled overland, led by Wilson Price Hunt, and the ship *Tonquin*, captained by Jonathan Thorn, was commissioned to sail to the Northwest Coast and establish trade with the Indian tribes. The crew of the *Tonquin* included a black cook whose name has not survived,[i] and two black men, Edward Rose and Francoise Duchouquette, were associated with Hunt's overland expedition.

Edward Rose, the son of a white trader among the Cherokee, was born in Kentucky. His mother was black and Cherokee. He spent much of his life among the Arikara and Crow tribes and became a Crow chief. His knowledge of the West and Indian tribes brought him opportunities as an interpreter, guide, and hunter with various expeditions. He spent several years with the fur trader and explorer Manuel Lisa, and helped to build Fort Raymond, located at the mouth of the Bighorn River in Montana.

Rose met Hunt in 1811, and was hired to guide the expedition to Oregon. He acquired the reputation of a troublemaker; Hunt described him as a "very bad fellow, full of daring," and suspected him of a plot to leave the expedition, taking some of his men to settle among the Crow Indians.[10] Hunt gave Rose enough provisions to last a year, and allowed him to leave the expedition in peace. Although Rose accompanied the expedition only as far as Montana, he mapped Hunt's passage farther to the west. Dismissing him may have been an unwise decision, as the party became lost along the Snake River, and several men nearly lost their lives before they reached the mouth of the Columbia and established Fort Astoria.

i The men were Francis Robertson (steward) and Thomas Williams (cook). See James P. Ronda, *Astoria and Empire* (Lincoln: University of Nebraska Press, 1993): 97.

In 1824 Edward Rose accompanied Jedediah Smith part of the way to South Pass. Although Smith was not the first white man to cross the pass, he was responsible for making it widely known as the best low pass through the Rockies that served thousands of immigrants coming overland to Oregon. Rose was also involved in an expedition with General Henry Atkinson, which came as far west as the Yellowstone region. Atkinson was assigned to make treaties with the hostile Missouri tribes, and Edward Rose acted as interpreter. He died in the 1830s in an Indian village.

Francoise Duchouquette was a Canadian trapper whose mother was a midwife of French and black ancestry, at the time the only woman at Prairie Du Chien who had any knowledge of medicine. He served Hunt's expedition as a blacksmith, and remained at Fort George (formerly Fort Astoria) until 1814, when the company left for Fort Williams, near Lake Superior. While in the Northwest he fathered a son, also named Francoise Duchouquette. His mother was an Okanogan Indian, he learned to read and write, and he was a storekeeper for the Hudson's Bay Company at Fort Okanogan from 1853 to 1860.[11]

Astor's plan to establish a profitable trading post suffered when the crew of the *Tonquin* was killed by hostile Indians during a trading expedition to Vancouver Island. A wounded sailor touched off the ammunition on the ship, and vessel, sailors and Indians were destroyed in the explosion that followed. In 1813, the Pacific Fur Company was sold to the North West Company, a Canadian fur trading corporation. American fur traders were never again active in Oregon, concentrating instead on the lucrative fur trade on the Missouri and in the Rocky Mountains.

A number of black men were associated with the Rocky Mountain fur trade, many as servants or slaves, or in menial positions as free laborers. It was not uncommon, however, to find blacks operating as independent trappers, guides and interpreters. Many had spent their lives living with Indians, and gained invaluable knowledge that served them well as negotiators with hostile tribes, and enabled them to survive the rigors of a wilderness life.

One of the most successful and famous of the black fur traders was James P. Beckwourth. Born in Virginia in 1798, his father was Sir Jennings Beckwith and his mother was a black woman. During his lifetime he made expeditions to Colorado, Nevada and California. He traveled extensively with William H. Ashley in the Rockies and as far west as the Yellowstone region. Like Rose, he lived with the Crow Indians for a time, and later became an influential citizen of Denver, Colorado. In 1851, he explored northern California and discovered a new route across the Sierras, a pass which bears his name. There is no evidence that he was ever in Oregon, but his explorations helped familiarize the major immigrant routes into the West.

During the decade of the 1830s, white people settled in Oregon, as Protestant churches began a campaign to convert the Indian tribes to Christianity. In 1836 the Whitman and Spalding families arrived in Oregon, bringing with them a black man named John Hinds. He had joined the party near the Green River at the 1836 fur traders' rendezvous in order to receive medical attention from Dr. Whitman, as he was suffering from dropsy. His condition did not improve and he died at the Whitman mission at Waiilatapu in November 1836. He was buried at the foot of a hill northeast of the mission house; Narcissa Whitman noted his death in a letter dated December 5, 1836: "Already death has entered our home and laid one low."[12]

Two black men are mentioned in missionary records for the year 1840. On May 21, the ship *Lausanne* anchored at the mouth of the Columbia River near Baker's Bay. On board were the Reverend John H. Frost and his family, Methodist missionaries sent to Oregon as part of Jason Lee's "Great Reinforcement." Lee, who had first come to Oregon in 1834, returned East to recruit more missionaries, hoping to develop an American community in the Willamette Valley, and strengthen American claims to the area. On the *Lausanne* were forty-nine missionaries and other settlers who came to live in Oregon.

The ship was piloted up the Columbia River to Fort Vancouver by several individuals, including a black man called George Washington. Little is known of this man, other than a few details noted by John Frost. Washington had been sent down river by John McLoughlin, with fresh bread and butter for the weary missionaries. Although the ship had been piloted by an Indian called Chinook George, he gave way when Washington produced a letter attesting to his abilities as a river pilot.

> Thus Chenook George (who called himself, at times, *King* George) was superceded in the pilot's office, which bid fair to blast his prospects of obtaining a reasonable fee from Captain Spaulding. However, determined to enjoy the privileges, he remained, sat down upon a spar, filled his pipe, and soon sank down into a state of unconsciousness, while George Washington took charge of the ship.
>
> We had not proceeded far when the vessel was brought up upon the sands, giving evidence that our pilot's knowledge was altogether inadequate. Upon this the old Indian awoke from his revery and stepped forward, with a smile of satisfaction beaming in his weather-beaten countenance, and said, "Me know George Washington one very good cook, but he no pilot." After the vessel was got off again into deep

> water, the charge was given to the old Chenook, who pointed out the channel in a very accurate manner.[13]

Frost's diary for the day also noted that the ship had run aground once before while in the river, and that progress toward Fort Vancouver was hampered by poor winds and bad weather.

In 1839 a black man called Wallace came to Oregon on board the brig *Maryland*, which had been sent from Boston on a trading expedition. The voyage was not entirely successful, although it returned with some of the first Columbia River salmon to be sent to the East Coast. While the *Maryland* was anchored in the Columbia, Wallace deserted. John Frost met Wallace and Calvin Tibbets in December 1840, at Fort George, where he had come for supplies. Frost was discouraged because of the dismal weather and poor progress on construction of the missionary settlement. Wallace and Tibbets went back to the settlement with Frost, helping to drag the supplies through waist-deep mud. They were hired to help construct a building near the banks of the Columbia. Wallace assisted in cutting the lumber and shingles for the house, and carried messages between the building site and the settlement further inland. Progress was slow in the damp Oregon winter. Once, Wallace was left alone at the building site, and when Frost returned he found him depressed and discouraged, as it had snowed the night before and was cold and dreary. This is the last mention of Wallace, and nothing is known of his fate.

A black man named Jacob Dodson came to Oregon in 1843 with Captain John Fremont. Dodson was a free servant in the family of Thomas Hart Benton, Fremont's father-in-law, and volunteered to accompany the expedition to Oregon. Nearly six feet tall and very strong, Dodson was only eighteen years old when he came to the West. Fremont valued his capabilities, and he was always included with the strongest men of the party who accompanied Fremont during the most difficult part of the trip. The expedition traveled from Fort Vancouver down the east side of the Cascade Mountains to Klamath Falls, exploring the region and mapping the geographic features. Jacob Dodson later became an attendant in the United States Senate, and at the outbreak of the Civil War raised 300 black men to fight for the Union, but President Lincoln refused their services.

In 1834, a black man named George Winslow came to Oregon with the famous trapper, Ewing Young, and an Oregon promoter, Hall Jackson Kelley. Kelley had studied the diaries of the Lewis and Clark Expedition, and although he had never seen Oregon, he published circulars which contained glowing descriptions of the area, emphasizing the fruitfulness of the land and the abundance of natural resources. Nothing is known of Winslow before he and eleven other men came from California to Oregon. He settled on the Clackamas Prairie, married an Indian woman, and raised a family. A knowledge of medicine supplemented his income, until the arrival of Dr. Forbes of the Hudson's Bay Company reduced his business.[j] He was best known to boast that he had come to Oregon not with Kelley, but with Astor's expedition on board the *Tonquin* in 1811.

Some time later Winslow moved farther north and raised potatoes and other produce on a farm which he sold to another black man, James D. Saules. Facts concerning his later life are vague, outside of his involvement in the "Cockstock Affair."[14] It was said that he moved to Clatsop County and lived near the mouth of the Columbia River. His name was mentioned in a newspaper article published in 1851 concerning the expulsion of Jacob Vanderpool from Oregon Territory under the exclusion law.

> A notorious villain, who calls himself Winslow, has cursed this community with his presence for a number of years. All manner of crimes have been laid to his charge. We shall rejoice at his removal.[15]

Although Winslow could not have been expelled from Oregon legally, his name vanished from the public record, and nothing is known of his fate.

James D. Saules came to Oregon with the U.S. Sloop-of-War *Peacock* in 1841. He served as a cook on the ship, and settled in Oregon City where he bought a farm from Winslow. A few months after the "Cockstock Affair" he ran into trouble with a white settler who accused him of stirring up the Indians against white settlers. Three witnesses testified against him, and he was found guilty. He was kept in custody for several weeks, but because there was no jail he was released and told to leave the area. He went to the Clatsop Plains near Astoria and worked at the Methodist Mission until 1846 when the mission was closed. Later, he was arrested and charged with causing the death of his Indian wife. A news article reported:

> A negro man named James D. Saules was brought to this city recently from the mouth of the river, charged with having caused the death of his wife, an Indian woman. He was examined before Justice Hood, the result of which examination we have never been able to ascertain, but the accused is at large and likely to remain so we suppose.[16]

---

j Winslow, or Anderson, provided medical care at the Methodist Mission at Wascopum, not in Clackamas Plains. "Dr. Forbes" is HBC surgeon Forbes Barclay. See Kenneth Robert Coleman, "'Dangerous Subjects': James D. Saules and the Enforcement of the Color Line in Oregon" (dissertations and theses, Portland State University, 2014).

He ran a ferry service between Astoria and Cathlamet, and once attempted to guide a ship across Chinook shoals, but his attempt was unsuccessful.[17] Although he ran afoul of the law occasionally, he was well liked. He was a musician and played the fiddle. He knew only a few songs, but had no rivals, and was in great demand at dances where he would play the same tunes over and over, to the delight of his audience.

He later lived in a cabin at Cape Disappointment facing Baker Bay. Peter Skene Ogden paid him $200 for his squatters rights to the property, intending to build a pilot's lookout and a British trading post on the site. Saules' name appears on the ledgers of the Cathlamet store in 1851, and two years later was on the list of the store's outstanding debtors.[18] It is speculated that he drowned in a boating accident in December 1851.

> We learn that three negro men have been engaged for some time past in selling liquor to Indians, a short distance from Milton, Washington county, and that the citizens of that place were so much annoyed by their continued drunkenness and debauchery, that several of the citizens started in a boat to take the negroes into custody. This they succeeded in doing, and when taking them before the Magistrate, by some means the boat was capsized, and one of the negroes drowned. For want of sufficient evidence to commit them, the other two were discharged.[19]

Beginning in the decade of the 1840s, the character of Oregon began to change. From a small and scattered population of fur traders and trappers, missionaries, Indians, British and American citizens, it was transformed into an American colony by the arrival of the wagon trains. Among those employees of the Hudson's Bay Company who experienced this change and the erosion of their influence was James C. Douglas, later Sir James Douglas, the first governor of British Columbia. He was born in the African colony of British Guiana in 1803.[k] His father was John Douglas, a Scottish merchant, and his mother was a creole woman named "Miss Ritchie." After his education in Scotland and England, he signed on with the North West Company and sailed from Liverpool to Canada at the age of sixteen. The North West Company merged with the Hudson's Bay Company in 1821, and four years later Douglas was transferred to Fort St. James, west of the Rockies. He was transferred again to Fort Vancouver in 1830, where he became the chief accountant.

There is some evidence to suggest that Douglas may have inherited some black ancestry from his mother. She was described as a creole, although that

k "British Guyana," today the nation of Guyana, is in South America, not Africa.

in itself would not necessarily signify that one of her parents was black, as in some Latin American countries creole could also mean a second generation European. Douglas was described as a "West Indian" by Governor George Simpson in 1832, and referred to as a mulatto by Letitia Hargrave in a letter written in 1842. Although it has not been established that James Douglas and Letitia Hargrave, the wife of a fur trader, ever met, her comment might reflect a common belief among fur traders concerning Douglas' racial identity.[20]

The Hudson's Bay Company often employed persons of mixed racial ancestry, and racial background was no detriment to advancement within the company. James Douglas' progress was noted in company correspondence for 1831. "James Douglas is at Vancouver and is rising fast in favor."[21] As chief accountant, he kept the company books and accompanied the annual trek east to Hudson Bay. In 1835, he was promoted to Chief Trader. He was left in charge of Fort Vancouver in 1838 and 1839, during the absence of Dr. John McLoughlin. In 1840 he was promoted to Chief Factor, the highest rank within the company.

The following year, he went on an expedition to California to establish a trading post at Yerba Buena, on the site of modern San Francisco. The growing number of American settlers prompted the closure of Yerba Buena, and the search for another site for company headquarters north of the Columbia River began. In 1842, Douglas explored the south coast of Vancouver Island and selected the site on which Fort Victoria was built in 1843.

The immigration of 1844 alone doubled the population of the Willamette Valley, and in 1845 Douglas and McLoughlin agreed to join the Provisional Government as representatives of the Hudson's Bay Company, to pay taxes on goods sold to settlers, and to comply with the laws passed by that body. Vancouver District was created to govern the area north of the Columbia River, and Douglas was elected to a three-year term as Judge.

Unlike McLoughlin, who was to leave the Hudson's Bay Company and settle in Oregon City, Douglas maintained his identity as a British citizen. As early as 1831 he predicted the consequences of a large migration of American settlers to Oregon.

> The interests of the [American] colony, and the Fur Trade will never harmonize, the former can flourish, only, through the protection of equal laws, the influence of free trade, the accession of respectable inhabitants; in short by establishing a new order of things, while the Fur Trade, must suffer by each innovation.[22]

He was often in the shadow of the older and more influential Chief Factor, and like McLoughlin, assisted settlers who arrived in Oregon penniless and without provisions. Peter Burnett met Douglas when he arrived at the Fort in 1843.

> Mr. James Douglas . . . was a younger man than Dr. McLoughlin by some fifteen years. He was a man of very superior intelligence, and a finished Christian gentleman. His course toward us was noble, prudent, and generous.[23]

McLoughlin was criticized by company officials for helping the American settlers who without his assistance, he claimed, could not have survived. Under the tenure of Douglas the practice of extending credit for the purchase of wheat was discontinued, to avoid similar criticism. By that time, wheat and flour could be purchased at mills in the Willamette Valley. In May of 1849, Douglas moved north to continue his career at Fort Victoria, at the end of the Hudson's Bay Company operations at Fort Vancouver.

Black people aided settlers on their way to Oregon from Independence, Missouri, which was described as "a great Babel upon the border of the wilderness."

> Here might be seen the African slave with his shining black face, driving his six horse team of blood-red bays, and swaying from side to side as he sat upon the saddle and listened to the incessant tinkling of the bells . . . some [wagons] driven by Spaniards, some by Americans resembling Indians, some by negroes, and others by persons of all possible crosses between these various races . . .[24]

A black man who lived in Missouri, Hiram Young, helped immigrants begin the journey. He owned wagon factories, blacksmith shops, and even slaves.

Moses Harris, black mountain man and wagon train guide, was by his own admission a native of Union County, South Carolina, although some sources state his birthplace was Kentucky.[25] After a long trapping and trading career which took him with Ashley's expeditions to the area near the headwaters of the Missouri and later as far west as Yellowstone between 1822 and 1826, he began to guide missionaries and wagon trains to Oregon. He was called "Black Harris," or the "Black Squire," and was described by the painter Alfred Jacob Miller, who also painted a portrait of him.

> This Black Harris always created a sensation at the campfire, being a capital *raconteur*, and having had as many perilous adventures as any

> man probably in the mountains. He was of wiry form, made up of bone and muscle, with a face apparently composed of tan leather and ship cord, finished off with a peculiar blue-black tint, as if gunpowder had been burnt into his face.[26]

His years in the mountains served him well in preparation for a career as a wagon train scout. One observer noted:

> It was said of him as early as 1823 that he was an "experienced mountaineer" . . . in whom the general [Ashley] reposed the strictest confidence for his knowledge of the country and his familiarity with Indian life. This Harris was reputed to be a man of "great leg" and capable from his long sojourning in the mountains, of enduring extreme privation and fatigue.[27]

His first contact with wagon trains was as a fur trader, while piloting supplies to the annual fur trader's rendezvous. In 1836, while on one trip, he escorted the Whitman and Spalding families as far west as the Green River. Two years later he escorted another missionary party as far as Fort Laramie, which he earlier had helped to locate and build.

By 1840, the declining fur trade meant the end of one career for Harris, and he offered his services to guide a group of immigrants to Fort Hall. His price was too high, and another guide was hired. He acted as guide for one of the largest immigrant trains to come to Oregon in 1844. The party, divided into three large sections, included a wealthy black man, George Bush, and Michael T. Simmons, John Minto, Nathaniel Ford and his family, and their black servants Robin, Polly and Mary Jane Holmes. They arrived in the Willamette Valley in October 1844, and Harris spent the winter there. He left the following spring with Elijah White, who was going east and wanted Harris to guide him. After Harris and White reached The Dalles, Harris decided to return to the Willamette Valley, but as he started back he met Stephen Meek, who was seeking help for a party of settlers stranded in central Oregon. The group had traveled south of the regular trail, trying to cross the Cascades by an old cutoff used by mountain men and trappers. They veered too far south, and became stranded in the desert. Called the "Blue Bucket" party because they picked up some nuggets which were forgotten until gold was discovered in California, more than twenty people died in the desert before Moses Harris rescued them. He secured supplies from Indians and guided them to The Dalles.

Several attempts were made to find a better route over the Cascades than Barlow Pass, which crossed over the mountains near Mt. Hood, and

Harris accompanied all these expeditions. A low pass in southern Oregon which was used by fur traders was located, and Harris accompanied Captain Levi Scott, and Jesse and Lindsay Applegate southeast to Fort Hall, and persuaded a party of settlers to try the new route. The first party suffered great hardships crossing over this pass, and it was widely criticized. It was called the Applegate Cutoff, and after initial difficulties it came to be used by many settlers.

Moses Harris remained in Oregon for about three years. His name was listed on the tax rolls of Yamhill County, and he signed a petition from the citizens of Yamhill County addressed to the Provisional Assembly, urging them to finance the construction of a public road in Oregon City. In the winter of 1846, he was again called upon to rescue stranded settlers, who were coming into Oregon across the Applegate Cutoff. Starting from his home near the Luckiamute River in early December with nine other men, Harris headed south with provisions and horses. Thomas Holt, who kept a diary of the trip, noted on December 8th,

> We met three families packing, and one family with a wagon. They tell us they have had nothing to eat today—the children are crying for bread. We let them have fifty pounds of flour. Traveled 4 miles through a mirey prairie and camped on a slough.[28]

The rescue party continued south, meeting families that had given up hope and could travel no farther without supplies and fresh horses. Some had not eaten bread for two months. Eventually, all the settlers were located, and Moses Harris returned to his home in mid-January. He left the Willamette Valley in the spring of 1847, returning to St. Joseph, Missouri, where he hoped to guide other settlers to Oregon. He placed a notice in the St. Joseph *Gazette* advertising his experience and knowledge of the West. He may have returned to Oregon that year, but it is unlikely, as he was back in St. Joseph in the spring of 1849. He obtained a contract to guide a party west that year, but traveled only as far as Independence, Missouri, where he became sick with cholera and died.

During his lifetime he had been a trapper and trader, fond of telling embellished tales around frontier campfires, and a strong advocate for the opening of the West to Americans. In 1841 he wrote a letter to Thornton Grimsley, offering to aid in the settlement of Oregon.

> Your name is well known in the mountains by many of our old friends who would be glad to join the standard of their country, and make a clean sweep of what is called the Origon Territory; that is to

> clear it of British and Indians. I was one of the seven hundred who invited you to take command and march through California, and will be with you if you can get the Government of the United States to authorize the occupancy of the Origon Country. I have been, as you know, twenty years in the mountains.[29]

According to the census taken in Oregon in 1850, 207 people were identified as black or mulatto. Of this number, three-quarters were actually Hawaiians or half-breed Indians, as the census takers tended to put all non-whites in the same category. There were actually only fifty-four black people included in the census of 1850.[30] Although many of the constitutions of the societies which sponsored wagon trains specifically excluded black people from joining them in the trip to Oregon, most black people came across the plains, many with white families as servants or slaves.[31] Some were promised freedom after arriving in Oregon. The majority of blacks living in Oregon were servants, laborers, or children living with white families. Most were poor and lacked the financial resources to establish independent households. They were further discouraged when in 1850 a federal decision barred them from claiming free land.

The Provisional Assembly proposed laws that allowed settlers to claim 640 acres of land, but these provisions required federal approval. Oregon sent its delegate to Congress to argue for free land, saying that the settlement of the area had helped to secure American claim to Oregon, and that the government should reward them. The bill presented by Oregon's representative, Samuel Thurston, proposed that 320 acres be granted to white men twenty-one and over, and an additional 320 acres to their wives if they were married, assuming that they had come to Oregon before December 1, 1850 and were married by December 1, 1851. Those arriving during the next three years would receive half that amount.

Some Congressmen opposed Thurston's proposal because blacks and other minorities were excluded, except the sons of white/Indian unions. Thurston argued that this provision was designed to discourage black people from coming to Oregon, where they might intermarry with Indians and threaten white control. Other Congressmen opposed the bill because they believe the land grants were too large to be cultivated by individual families, and a sparse population and land speculation would result. Thurston was able to overcome these oppositions, and the bill passed without modification. The Oregon Donation Land Act, with its promise of free land for white settlers only, became law in September 1850.

Among those who arrived in Oregon Territory in 1844 was a black man named George Bush and his family. Unlike most of the other blacks who came to Oregon, Bush was a man of wealth, and even aided other needy families on the trip west. The date and place of his birth are disputed, but according to the family history he was born in Pennsylvania in 1779. His father, Matthew Bush, was born in India and was brought to the United States as a servant of a Captain Stevenson. His mother was Irish, and was a maid in the Stevenson household According to one observer, his descendants show no trace of his black heritage, and there are no pictures of him.[32] While his ethnic heritage may be disputed, he was racially identified as a black person by his contemporaries. John Minto recalled a conversation with Bush while on the Oregon Trail in 1844.

> I struck the road again in advance of my friends near Soda Springs. There was in sight, however, G. W. Bush, at whose camp . . . I had received the hospitality of the Missouri rendezvous. Joining him we went on to the springs. Bush was a mulatto, but had means, and also a white woman for a wife and a family of five children. Not many men of color left a slave state so well to do, and so generally respected; but it was not in the nature of things that he should be permitted to forget his color. As we went along together, he riding a mule and I on foot, he led the conversation to this subject. He told me that he should watch, when we got to Oregon, what usage was awarded to people of color, and if he could not have a free man's rights he would seek the protection of the Mexican government in California or New Mexico. He said there were few in that train he would say as much to as he had just said to me. I told him l understood.[33]

Ezra Meeker, another friend of Bush, said that he had left Missouri "because of the virulent prejudice against his race in the community where he lived."[34]

Bush had lived in Tennessee, Illinois and in Missouri for over twenty years. He had also been employed by the Hudson's Bay Company, and may have visited the Far West in the 1820s. In 1832 he married Isabella James and they raised a family of boys, five of whom survived beyond infancy. Bush left Missouri as a middle-aged man of wealth; stories were told of the false bottom in one of his wagons that concealed over $2,000 in silver coins. The crossing to Oregon was full of the usual problems of scarce food and water, and heavy rains delayed the party so that they arrived at The Dalles late in the fall of 1844. Bush spent the winter on the south side of the Columbia River near The Dalles, tending the livestock. Michael Simmons, his friend and partner, spent the next spring and summer exploring the Puget Sound area, and in October 1845, the two men and their families left The Dalles and settled on good farmland near modern Tumwater, Washington. Oregon had declared its prejudice against black people by passing the first of the exclusion laws in 1844, but the law could not be enforced in the wilderness north of the Columbia River. Bush enjoyed a free man's rights in that unsettled country, in an area still called Bush Prairie, and helped to secure American claim to modern Washington State.

The first years were hard, complicated by severe winters, but the Bush family prospered, raising wheat and vegetables. Isabella raised poultry and sheep, and seeds of fruit trees brought from Missouri soon began to bear fruit. The family's reputation for kindness and generosity were well known. One year, wheat was in short supply and Bush was offered an unheard-of price for his entire crop. His response was not forgotten.

> I'll just keep my grain to let my neighbors who have had failures have enough to live on and for seeding their fields in the spring. They have no money to pay your fancy prices and I don't intend to see them want for anything in my power to provide them with.[35]

Washington was organized as a separate Territory in 1853. Under the provision of the Donation Land Act, Bush could not legally claim title to the 640 acres of land he had settled and farmed since 1845, because he was a black man. His white friends did not forget him, and the first legislative assembly passed a petition on his behalf, urging that Congress pass a special act giving George Bush title to his land. The following year this was approved.

Black people shared the pioneering spirit that transformed Oregon from a wilderness into a thriving American territory. They came because of special talents, an accident of fate, or by deliberate efforts to enjoy a freer life. A few participated in the early expeditions that provided the information that changed the image of Oregon from an unknown wilderness into a rich agricultural paradise in the West. Others by individual efforts helped to create a thriving community. The first indications that this was not to be an unblemished land of promise for black people began to appear in the decade of the 1840s as the pioneer government passed laws designed to discourage black people from making a new life in Oregon.

2

To Keep Clear of this Most Troublesome Class

The Exclusion Laws 1844–1857

On August 20, 1851, a black man named Jacob Vanderpool, who owned a saloon, restaurant and boarding house across the street from the offices of the *Oregon Statesman* in Salem,[a] was arrested and jailed. His crime was living illegally in Oregon because he was black. Theophilus Magruder had filed a complaint against him, saying that his residence in Oregon was illegal because of an exclusion law passed by the Territorial government in 1849. Five days later, Vanderpool was brought to trial. His defense lawyer argued that the law was unconstitutional since it had not been legally approved by the legislature. The prosecution produced three witnesses who verified the date of Vanderpool's arrival in Oregon. All three were vague. A verdict was rendered the following day, and Judge Thomas Nelson ordered Jacob Vanderpool to leave Oregon.

> I being satisfied that the same Jacob Vanderpool is a mulatto and that he is remaining in the territory of Oregon contrary to the Statutes and laws of the territory, do therefore order that the said Jacob Vanderpool remove from said territory within thirty days from and upon the service of this order—the said order to be served by showing to the said Jacob Vanderpool this original and at the same time delivering to him a true copy of the same.[1]

The decision was delivered to him the same day by the sheriff of Clackamas County. The *Oregon Spectator* commented:

a Vanderpool's saloon was located in Oregon City. This discrepancy comes from an August 8, 1851, newspaper advertisement that states the location of Vanderpool's saloon as "opposite the *Statesman* office." From its founding in 1851 until 1853, the *Oregon Statesman* was published in Oregon City. The paper moved to Salem in 1855.

> There is a statute prohibiting the introduction of negroes into Oregon. A misdemeanor committed by one Vanderpool was the cause of bringing this individual before his Honor Judge Nelson, and a decision was called for respecting the enforcement of that law; who decided that the statute should be immediately enforced and that the negro shall be banished forth with from the Territory.[2]

Jacob Vanderpool was the first and only black person of record to be expelled from Oregon because of his race.

From the beginning of governmental organization in Oregon the question of slavery and the rights of free black people were discussed and debated. Slavery existed, although consistently prohibited by law.[3] Exclusion laws designed to prevent black people from coming to Oregon were passed twice during the 1840s, considered several times and finally passed as part of the state constitution in 1857. The takeover of Indian lands prompted hostility between Indians and whites; the "Cockstock Affair" raised fears that without an exclusion law settlers might have two hostile minority groups to deal with.

The people who settled in Oregon tended to come from the frontier areas of the Middle West, particularly the Ohio and Mississippi River valleys. The move West for many included the expectation that they could settle in an area untroubled by racial concerns. R. W. Morrison, who crossed the plains in 1844, gave his reasons for coming to Oregon in a conversation recorded by John Minto.

> Well, I allow the United States has the best right to that country, and I am going to help make that right good . . . Then, I am not satisfied here. There is little we raise that pays shipment to market; a little hemp and a little tobacco. Unless a man keeps niggers (and I won't) he has no even chance; he cannot compete with the man that does . . . I'm going to Oregon, where there'll be no slaves, and we'll all start even.[4]

Laws restricting the rights of black people were not an original idea in Oregon, nor were they unknown outside the South. In the first fifty years of the nineteenth century Ohio, Illinois, Indiana and Missouri had passed laws restricting the rights of black people. These laws denied them the vote, restricted free access into the territory, restricted testimony in court, required the posting of bonds for good behavior, demanded that black people carry proof of freedom, or excluded them altogether from living in these territories. Exclusion laws similar to those enacted in Oregon were passed in Indiana and Illinois and considered, though never passed, in Ohio. Familiar with laws passed in other frontier areas and desirous of keeping Oregon free from troublesome racial questions, settlers who brought racist attitudes with them across the plains saw legal restrictions as the best solution to the problem.

The Organic Code of the provisional government adopted in 1843 prohibited slavery and restricted voting rights to free male descendants of white men twenty-one years of age or older, effectively excluding all black and most Indian men.[b] Between the meetings of the provisional government of 1843 and 1844 an event took place that raised the fear of black and Indian hostility and prompted the passage of more severe restrictions on the freedom of black people. This incident, called the "Cockstock Affair," took place in Oregon City in March 1844.

A black man named George Winslow, also known as Winslow Anderson, had hired an Indian named Cockstock to clear a tract of land on his farm near Oregon City. Cockstock was to receive a horse when the job was completed. Winslow meanwhile sold the horse and the farm to James D. Saules, and when Cockstock finished the job and asked for payment, Saules refused to give him the horse. Vowing vengeance against both black men, Cockstock stole the horse. When Elijah White, the local Indian agent, compelled Cockstock to return the horse, he renewed his threats against the two men. White finally offered a $100 reward, hoping that Cockstock could be taken peaceably, but this only enraged him to an armed confrontation. He and two bystanders were killed, and several other men were wounded.

Elijah White feared the outbreak of an Indian war, and reported the incident to the Secretary of War, saying,

> I believe it morally impossible for us to remain at peace in Oregon, for any considerable time, without the protection of vigorous civil or military law.[5]

The Legislative Committee met five days later, mourning the loss of their clerk, George LeBreton, who was killed during the incident. The immediate result was the formation of the Oregon Rangers, the first military organization in Oregon. A few months later, the first exclusion law was proposed.[c]

b It should be noted that Oregon's provisional government was a loose form of self-governance with no authority recognized by the United States or Great Britain. Settlers were under no obligation to abide by any laws passed by this body, and there were no mechanisms for enforcement. This is what allowed slavery to exist in Oregon despite laws barring it, and what allowed a few free Blacks to come to Oregon despite the 1844 Black exclusion law. See Barbara Mahoney, "Provisional Government," Oregon Encyclopedia (2020).

c The cause and effect of the Cockstock incident and the passage of the 1844 Black exclusion law are not as certain as is suggested here. It was only after Saules was convicted of conspiring to burn down the home of his white neighbor, Charles Pickett, (two months after the Oregon City events) and was

The exclusion law, passed on June 26, 1844, repeated the anti-slavery law passed in 1843 and required all blacks to leave the territory within three years. Slaveowners were required to free their slaves, who were included in the expulsion order.[d] Anyone in violation of the law would suffer a whip lashing, to be repeated after six months if they still refused to leave.

When the Committee met in December 1844, two members urged that the exclusion law be modified so that black people might remain if they posted a bond for good behavior. The act was amended, substituting a term of hard labor for the whip lashing, but black people were still required to leave. This law was designed to take effect in 1846, was repealed in 1845, and thus never directly enforced.

Four years later, another attempt to pass an exclusion law was successful, this time in effect long enough to force Jacob Vanderpool out of Oregon. By 1849, when Oregon was organized as a territory, the population had grown dramatically, and increasing settlement on Indian lands led to conflict. Two years earlier, in November of 1847, Dr. and Mrs. Marcus Whitman and twelve other white people were murdered by Cayuse braves at their mission at Waiilatapu on the Walla Walla River. For more than two years the Indians involved were pursued until they surrendered and were hanged at Oregon City. Although no black people were involved in this incident, racist legislation was again seen as a cure for white anxieties.[e] The preamble to the exclusion bill introduced in September 1849 stated:

> . . . situated as the people of Oregon are, in the midst of an Indian population, it would be highly dangerous to allow free negroes and mulattoes to reside in the territory or to intermix with the Indians, instilling in their minds feelings of hostility against the white race . . . be it enacted . . . that it shall not be lawful for any negro or mulatto to come in or reside within the limits of this Territory.[6]

This bill permitted black settlers and their children who were already living in Oregon to stay, but prohibited other black people from moving

banished from the Willamette Valley that Indian Subagent Elijah White wrote to US Secretary of War William Wilkins and suggested that all Blacks be deported or barred from entry. See Coleman for more.

d Under Sections II and IV of this law, slaveowners had up to three years before they were required to emancipate their enslaved property; two years for Black men and three years for Black women.

e Elizabeth Sager Helm survived the massacre and recalled the experience to Fred Lockley of the *Oregon Daily Journal* for serialized publication in May 1915. In her recollections, she names a Canadian "half-breed Negro" named Joe Lewis as one of the primary instigators of the massacre. Lewis comes up in other sources, though most refer to him only as "half-breed" or "half breed Indian" without elaborating further.

in. It included provisions to prevent blacks from coming to Oregon by ship. Ship owners were responsible for seeing that all black crew members left the territory with their ship. A $500 fine was the penalty for a negligent ship owner. Any black person in violation of the law was to be arrested and ordered to leave. The bill was passed September 21, 1849.

During the five years the law was in force, petitions were presented to the legislature on behalf of several black citizens, requesting that the law be repealed. The first was presented in 1851, on behalf of A. H. and O. B. Francis, residents of Portland.[f]

> We the undersigned citizens of the Territory of Oregon, in view of an existing law passed . . . in September of 1849 prohibiting Negroes or Mulattoes from settling in the Territory, beg leave to call your attention to the severity of this law, and the injustice often resulting from the enforcement of it. There are frequently coming into the Territory a class of men to whom this law will apply. They have proved themselves to be moral, industrious, and civil. Having no knowledge of this law some of them have spent their all by purchasing property, or entering into business to gain an honest living. We see and feel this injustice done them, by more unworthy and designing men lodging complaint against them under this law, and they thus ordered at great sacrifice to leave the Territory. We humbly ask your Honourable body, to repeal or so modify this law that all classes of honest and industrious men may have an equal chance.[7]

The petitioners argued that the danger of combined Indian and black hostilities against white people no longer existed, and they requested that a special law be passed allowing A. H. and O. B. Francis to remain in Oregon.

The same year a petition was presented on behalf of George Washington. One of the founders of Centralia, Washington, he had settled in the area, still a part of Oregon Territory, in 1850. A third petition was presented in 1854 on behalf of Morris Thomas, another black resident of Portland. All three petitions took the form of general bills to repeal the exclusion law, and all were defeated. Washington was organized as a separate territory in 1853, and the area north of the Columbia River passed out of the jurisdiction of Oregon's territorial legislature. No record of court proceedings to expel anyone other than Jacob Vanderpool has been located.

During extensive revisions of territorial laws accomplished in 1854, a general repealing act was passed voiding all previous legislation except

f The brothers were Abner, or A. H., Francis and Isaac, or I. B., Francis.

certain specified laws. The 1849 exclusion law was not on this list, and thus was repealed. Later attempts to revive the law suggest that its omission was accidental.

In the winter of 1856–57, debates on slavery and the rights of black people were widespread in the local press, and another attempt was made to pass an exclusion law. One legislator, arguing in favor of the law, said black settlers had no right to stay in Oregon because they had taken no part in settling the area and defeating the Indians. Opponents of the bill spoke of its injustice, and pointed out that clauses penalizing ship owners for blacks who jumped ship in Oregon could hurt the shipping trade, and said further that the proposed law was merely a tactic intended to stir up public opinion. Another opponent was quoted as saying,

> What negroes we have in the country it is conceded are law abiding, peaceable, and they are not sufficiently numerous to supply the barber's shops and kitchens of the towns . . . If a man wants his boots blacked he must do it himself.[8]

This exclusion bill passed in the Senate, but was defeated in the House. The territorial legislature did not again attempt to pass an exclusion law, but the idea was not abandoned. In 1857, the men who wrote Oregon's constitution proposed that the voters of Oregon should decide if they wanted an exclusion clause in the state constitution. An exclusion clause was approved by popular vote in 1857, and remained as a part of Oregon's constitution long after nullification by the Civil War amendments to the federal Constitution. The clause was not repealed until 1926.

The idea of the exclusion of black people was odious to some Oregonians, particularly in the 1840s and early 1850s, when most believed themselves remote from pressing racial issues in the East. This minority, who signed petitions and favored repeal of the law, included a well known settler, Jesse Applegate. He came to Oregon in 1843, was elected to the Legislative Committee, and supported the repeal of the 1844 exclusion law in 1845. Applegate was born in Kentucky and later moved to Missouri, where he farmed in the Osage Valley. He refused to own slaves, although he could afford them, and at times was forced to hire slaves from neighboring farms when free labor was scarce. His opposition to the exclusion law was uncharacteristic of the economic class with which he identified.

> Being one of the "Poor Whites" from a slave state I can speak with some authority for that class—Many of those people hated slavery,

> but a much larger number of them hated *free negroes* worse even than slaves . . .[9]

Another influential settler, Peter Burnett, had the exclusion of blacks in mind when he came to Oregon. His letters were published in Missouri newspapers, and his descriptions of Oregon encouraged many others to move West. In one letter he wrote:

> The object is to *keep* clear of this most troublesome class of population. We are in a new world, under most favorable circumstances, and we wish to avoid most of these great evils that have so much afflicted the United States and other countries.[10]

His past experience was typical of a common pattern of westward migration. The eldest of eight children, he was born in Tennessee and moved to Missouri with his family, where he recalled,

> We spent the first winter in a large camp with a dirt floor, boarded up on the sides with clapboards and covered with the same, having a hole in the center of the roof for the escape of smoke. All the family lived together in the same room, the whites on one side and the blacks on the other.[11]

Never attending school, he was self-educated and studied law. He operated a general store in Missouri, and in 1830 was responsible for the death of a black man who he claimed had stolen liquor from his store. He was acquainted with Moses Harris, and used to repeat the famous yarn that Harris told about the petrified forests in the Black Hills.

Burnett came to Oregon with his family in 1843, and settled on a farm near Hillsboro, where he represented the district of Tualatin on the Legislative Committee of 1844 and introduced the exclusion law passed in that session. He later attempted to justify this exclusion law, arguing that emigration was a privilege, not an inherent right, and that this privilege could be denied to a particular class or race of people without denying them constitutional rights. Since blacks were not permitted to vote, he argued, it was better to deny them residence as well, since they would have no motive for self-improvement. Burnett declared that if he could have predicted the Civil War he would not have supported such a law, and as it was later modified no one should be blamed for supporting it.[12]

He did not seek election to the Committee of 1845, and moved to California in 1848. After mining gold for a time, he moved to San Francisco and again became involved in politics, where he continued to support racist legislation. He was elected the first state governor in 1850, and in his inaugural message proposed an exclusion law. He had been preceeded to California by another ex-Oregonian, M. M. McCarver, who voted for the exclusion law in Oregon and proposed that a similar law be included in California's constitution. Burnett's proposal was defeated, as was McCarver's, but in 1858, as Chief Justice of the state Supreme Court, Burnett ruled that an ex-slave, Archy Lee, was legally the property of his former master. Although a lower court had given Lee his freedom, Burnett reversed this decision, saying the anti-slavery law was:

> . . . merely directional . . . This is the first case that has occurred under the existing law . . . under these circumstances we are not disposed to rigidly enforce the rules for the first time. But in reference to all future cases, it is our purpose to enforce the rules laid down strictly, according to their true intent and spirit.[13]

This decision and other racist legislation pending in the California legislature so enraged some members of the black community of San Francisco that several hundred decided to leave the state. Bypassing Oregon and Washington territories, they settled in Vancouver, British Columbia, at the invitation of James C. Douglas.[g]

The immediate justification of the exclusion laws passed in 1844 and 1849 was the fear of combined black/Indian hostilities, a paranoia that found frequent expression in the documents of the day. Samuel Thurston, delegate to Congress in 1850, repeated the same fear in his efforts to secure the restriction of land grants to white people only.

> The first legislative assembly that met last July, passed another law against the introduction of free negroes. This is a question of life and death to us in Oregon, and of money to this Government. The negroes associate with the Indians and intermarry, and, if their free ingress is encouraged or allowed there would a relationship spring up between them and the different tribes, and a mixed race would ensue inimical to the whites; and the Indians being led on by the negro who is better acquainted with the customs, language, and manners of the whites, than the Indian, these savages would become much more formidable than they otherwise would, and long and bloody wars would be

g The Black California immigrant community was in Victoria, on Vancouver Island, and British Columbia's Gulf Islands. Non-Indigenous settlement in what is today Vancouver did not begin until 1862. See James William Pilton, "Negro Settlement in British Columbia: 1858–1871" (dissertations and theses, University of British Columbia, 1951).

> the fruits of the comingling of the races. It is the principle of self-preservation that justifies the action of the Oregon legislature.[14]

The exclusion laws lasted long after Indian and black hostilities were even a remote possibility. Anti-black sentiment in Oregon was apparent from the beginning, and an exclusion clause remained on the books, despite repeated efforts to have it removed, until 1926.

3

To Hold Slaves in Oregon

The Slavery Debates 1850–1857

Robin and Polly Holmes and their three-year-old daughter Mary Jane arrived in Oregon Territory in 1844. Typical of the way many black people came to Oregon during this time, they traveled overland in the company of another black man, Scott, as slaves of Nathaniel Ford and his family.

Little is known of their earlier life. According to Robin's court testimony, they had been slaves of a Major Whitman, an army paymaster in Howard County, Missouri. In 1841, when Nathaniel Ford was sheriff of that county, they were sold to pay their master's debts. Never delivered to their new master, they became the slaves of the Ford family. In 1844 Ford was in financial difficulties and moved to Oregon. Robin believed that by helping his master establish himself he would eventually earn his freedom and that of his family. While living with Ford in Oregon, Robin and Scott raised vegetables to sell to the neighbors. Three more children were born to Robin and Polly Holmes: a son, James, in 1845, a daughter, Roxanna, in 1847, and a son, Lon, in 1850.[a]

In 1849, Robin asked for his freedom. Ford requested that he go to the California gold fields with Mark Ford, promising him freedom and a share of the gold when they returned. Robin agreed and went to California, where he served as camp cook. He also mined gold worth $900. On the return trip, Mark Ford and Scott were drowned.

In 1850, Robin and Polly and their infant son Lon moved five miles away to a house near Nesmith's Mills. Ford refused to allow Mary Jane, James and Roxanna to leave with their parents. Two years later, Robin, a poor and uneducated man, but mindful that Oregon was free territory, began a long legal battle to regain custody of his children.

---

a Other sources indicate that the Holmeses came west with three children: Mary Jane, James, and Roxanna. Lon and a daughter named Harriet (who died in 1851) were born in Oregon. See R. Gregory Nokes, *Breaking Chains: Slavery on Trial in the Oregon Territory* (Corvallis: Oregon State University Press, 2013).

Ford was served with a summons to appear at the next term of the District Court in April 1852, to answer the charge that he was holding the Holmes children unlawfully. The case was not heard until one year later, when Ford and Holmes appeared in court to present their arguments. Ford claimed that he was the legal owner of Robin, Polly, and Mary Jane, and that he had brought them to Oregon as his slaves. He argued that James and Roxanna were his wards by an agreement he made with Robin after his return from California, which gave him custody of Mary Jane and Roxanna until they were eighteen, and James until he was twenty-one. Ford said he had raised the children at great expense when they were too young to be of any value to him, and now he had a right to their services as compensation. He claimed he could take the family back to Missouri and sell them as slaves. He said finally that the children would suffer if they were to live with their parents, as Robin was poor, ignorant, and unfit to care for them.

Robin told the court the circumstances under which he and his wife became Ford's slaves, repeated Ford's promise of freedom in Oregon, and related the circumstances which led him to seek legal redress against his former master. He said that whenever he asked Ford for his freedom, Ford threatened to take the family back to Missouri and sell them. Robin denied the agreement concerning his children, and said he was able to support them.

The judge, Cyrus Olney, ruled that Ford must bring the children to the court, where they would be held until their status was decided. He failed to bring them to a hearing in April 1853, promising instead to give Holmes a $3,000 bond to guarantee that the children would not be taken out of Oregon. He requested a delay until Joseph Lane, witness to the agreement about the children, could return to Oregon to testify. Lane was then in Washington, D.C.

Two months later, Holmes renewed his petition to the courts. He feared that the children were mistreated and that Ford intended to send them back to Missouri. He complained of the long delay and the reluctance of the presiding judge to make a decision. Cyrus Olney ruled that Ford must release the children either to the court or to the local sheriff. Ford ignored this court order and, two weeks later at the next court appearance, the children were still in his custody.

Justice Olney attempted to postpone the case for another six months. In the meantime, he ruled that Mary Jane would be free either to stay with Ford or to go to her parents. He awarded temporary custody of Roxanna to Ford, and James to his father. Both were required to post a $1,000 bond to insure that the children would be produced at the trial date.

Robin, being poor, did not have the bond money, and remained dissatisfied with the delaying tactics of the judge. He presented his case to Justice George H. Williams, who had just arrived in Oregon, appointed chief justice of the Supreme Court of Oregon Territory by President Zachary Taylor.

Joseph Lane presented his testimony to the court, but his recollections were vague. He remembered offering a job to Robin and Polly and that his offer had led to the conversation with Ford concerning the children. Lane was only able to say that he was left with the impression that the children were to remain with Ford.

Two days after Justice Williams heard the evidence in the case, he awarded full custody of the three children to their parents and the family was reunited. How close they came to a permanent separation is indicated in a letter Nathaniel Ford wrote to a friend in Missouri, a year before the case was finally decided.

> You know I brought some negroes with me to this country which has proved a curse to me . . . Robin and his wife done verry well untill the spring of '50 when the abolitionists interfered –and the country is full of them—the interference was so great that I had to let them go . . . you know Crigler the sheriff had leveyed an execution on the negroes and they were brought off to this country. I am of the opinion that the execution may be so renewed as to send it here and take the negroes back to Missouri under the fugitive slave law . . . Robin and his wife Polly are very likely—they have five likely children if you can make the arrangement you may make some 1500 to 2000$ out of them and do me a great favor. If the negroes can be taken under the fugitive slave law I will make the arrangements to send them to you in short order . . . if the case of the negroes can be attended to it will releave me and my family of much trouble and you may be benefitted by it . . . I should like if there can anything be done to have the writ here by the first of October next—that is the time of the setting of our district court.[1]

Williams' written decision does not reveal the legal grounds for his decision, nor did it cite earlier anti-slavery laws as the legal basis for freeing the children. Later, he was to reveal his reasoning.

> Whether or not slaveholders could carry their slaves into the territories and hold them there as property had become a burning question, and my predecessors in office, for reasons best known to themselves, had declined to hear the case . . . I so held, that *without*

> *some positive legislative establishing slavery here,* it did not and could not exist in Oregon, and I awarded the colored people their freedom . . . So far as I know, this was the last effort made to hold slaves in Oregon *by force of law.* There were a great many pro-slavery men in the territory, and this decision, of course, was very distasteful to them.[2]

The decision was based on a strict interpretation of the law, using essentially the same arguments proposed by Senator Stephen O. Douglas, Williams' personal and political friend, and did not establish a precedent for further anti-slavery legislation. In 1857, Williams publicly admitted that he had no moral or ethical objections to slavery. Echoing Peter Burnett's sentiments, he proposed to stay as far away from this troublesome issue as possible.[3] The reluctance of other judges to rule on this case is one indication of how complex the issue of slavery had become in the ten years that intervened between the passage of the first anti-slavery law in 1843 and the decision that gave the Holmes children their freedom.

In early 1843, a temporary government evolved out of local meetings held to discuss the control of predatory animals. These "Wolf Meetings" evolved into a Legislative Committee which began to draft a code of laws for the government of the region. Hoping to be annexed by the United States and mindful of the Ordinance of 1787 which had been invoked to exclude slavery from northern U. S. territories in the Midwest, the Legislative Committee proposed an anti-slavery law, based on the Northwest Ordinance. This was approved in June 1843. No opposition was recorded, but evidence presented in a legislative session fourteen years later suggests that the law was not always observed.[4]

The boundary between the United States and Canada was settled in 1846, and Oregon became a part of the United States. By 1848, when it was officially organized as a territory, Oregonians had witnessed the first of a number of congressional debates in which the status of Oregon was linked with the slavery issue. Already, Oregonians who were isolated and free from local conditions that required a discussion of slavery were drawn into the controversy.

The bill to create Oregon Territory was coupled with the Wilmot Proviso, which required that any territory acquired from Mexico be free. David Wilmot, the author of the bill, believed that Congress possessed the power to regulate slavery in the territories, and should use it for total exclusion. He wanted to bring the issue of slavery in the territories to a final resolution. Other formulas on slavery more favorable to southern interests were evolving, and southern Senators, hoping to maintain a balance between slave and free territories, hoped to trade the admission of Oregon as free territory for the defeat of the Wilmot Proviso.

John C. Calhoun, one southern Senator, argued that Congress had the responsibility to protect the property of all citizens. Since slaves were property, Congress could not prohibit slavery in any territory, as it would deny to a portion of its citizens their fundamental right to travel to any territory with their slave property. A proposal to let the courts decide the status of slavery in the territories indicated the depth of disagreement developing in Congress. A proposal to extend the Missouri Compromise line to the Pacific Ocean was offered by Stephen O. Douglas. It included a more specific admission that slavery would be allowed south of the line, but was defeated by northern Congressmen anxious to win the support of the newly organized, anti-slavery Free Soil party.

The Wilmot Proviso was defeated after much debate, and there was no resolution of the issue of slavery in the territories. The Oregon Bill was adopted with an anti-slavery clause. Oregon was to be free, but only during territorial status. Statehood was inevitable, and would occasion another series of debates over slavery.

Territorial status meant that Oregonians were no longer free to elect their leaders; officials were now appointed by the federal government. Jesse Applegate voiced the frustration of Oregonians over their lack of self government in a letter critical of the kind of officials being appointed to govern Oregon.

> It really appears Mr. Fillmore considers Oregon as a kind of Botany Bay to which he banishes all the worthless needy and recreant of his party, with us they have no fellow feeling and so they appear to consider their life short [and] are determined to make use of every moment of it to fill their pockets. I have been agrieved by some of them but I shall make no complaint, nor tell tales unless in self-defense...[5]

Ironically, a doctrine concerning slavery called popular sovereignty provided Oregonians with a formula that best suited their desire to retain control of local government and their dissatisfaction with federal interference in local affairs.

First formulated by Lewis Cass of Michigan in his "Nicholson letter," written in December 1847, the doctrine of popular sovereignty attempted to provide a solution to the extension of slavery into the territories by declaring that the issue should be decided by each territory in a popular election. The doctrine was ambiguous because it did not specify at which point in the process of organization the territories would be allowed to put the issue to a vote. This ambiguity lent itself to a favorable interpretation by both northern and southern Democrats. Northern Democrats could promise that popular sovereignty would allow pioneer legislatures to keep their territory free, and southern Democrats could predict that this doctrine would allow slavery to establish a foothold in a territory before the question was settled by a vote at the end of territorial status.

The doctrine was further confused in the minds of Oregonians by the peculiar meaning they attached to it. Untroubled by a serious threat that slavery would be supported by the majority of voters, they pushed the doctrine to its logical conclusion. Not only should territories be allowed to decide the question of slavery, but all other local issues as well.

> To them it meant the fulfillment of their hopes and demands for complete self-government, for election of all territorial officers. It meant the end of imported officials.[6]

Offered as an alternative solution during the Oregon debates of 1848, the doctrine was first applied to the territories of Utah and New Mexico in 1850. The privilege of popular sovereignty was granted to the rest of the western territories including Oregon, in the Kansas-Nebraska Act, passed by Congress in 1854. The bill was sponsored by Stephen O. Douglas, who was primarily interested in a scheme for a western railway system. He was able to gain support for his bill by pointing out to southern Senators that slavery would now be possible in any area of the West. The Kansas-Nebraska Act was intended to provide a permanent solution to the problem of slavery in the territories, but its results were far different than Douglas imagined. He was reputedly opposed to the extension of slavery, although favoring the preservation of the Union over the abolition of slavery. After the bill was passed, he was permanently discredited in the minds of anti-slavery supporters, the doctrine was contaminated by pro-slavery implications, and a strong reaction against slavery split the national Democratic party.

In Oregon, the Kansas-Nebraska Act was praised as an end to federal interference in local affairs. It was the subject of a resolution introduced in the Oregon legislature by Delazon Smith, who also declared that the act implied an automatic repeal of Oregon's anti-slavery law. He added, however, that he believed that slavery would never be legalized in Oregon because of adverse economic conditions and local opposition. R. J. Ladd proposed an amendment to Smith's resolution which would prevent discrimination against anyone wishing to bring and hold slaves in Oregon. His amendment was narrowly defeated.

Clearly, at first the bill was applauded for its wider implications of local control of government. The polarization of beliefs on slavery which split the national Democratic party took more time to develop in Oregon, but as it developed the local party fostered a planned policy of silence on slavery in order to maintain party unity.

The Democratic party had been organized in Oregon in 1852. The party with which most Oregon settlers identified, it quickly dominated local politics. It was strengthened by the presence of Joseph Lane, the appointed territorial governor and a Democrat himself, who had adapted himself to local interests and was widely admired as a veteran of the Mexican War. Well known as a Southerner, he was sympathetic to slave-owning interests, but in the 1850s remained silent on the subject of slavery.

Party leadership centered around a nucleus of powerful men, primarily interested in the pursuit of high office and control over the distribution of political spoils. Dubbed the "Salem Clique" by its critics, the group included Asahel Bush, publisher of the *Oregon Statesman;* Delazon Smith, James W. Nesmith, R. P. Boise, and Lafayette Grover. All were later to be appointed or elected to high public office.[7]

Quick to applaud the doctrine of popular sovereignty, primarily as it offered more political power to the local party, the Democratic leadership downplayed the slavery issue, hoping to avoid the divisive effects of controversy that had weakened their national organization. Discussion of slavery by free state Democrats was equated with slavery agitation, labeled "Black Republican" or "abolitionist," and slavery agitation meant disloyalty to the party. As one observer of the political scene recalled,

> According to the theory of squatter sovereignty, a Democrat might vote for or against slavery, when a Territory is emerging to statehood; he could express his individual opinion by ballot at this time, but he could not promulgate it and give the reason for it or try to influence others and maintain his standing as a Democrat. If he did, he was thereafter considered a heretic, out of line of promotion or patronage, a punishment the dullest Democrat could feel and understand.[8]

Many of the leaders of the Democratic party were pro-slavery by reputation. This planned silence worked to their advantage, effectively forbidding a anti-slavery wing to establish itself within the party and relieving them of the need to defend or define their own position concerning slavery for Oregon.

By 1857, when the agitation over slavery had reached its height in Oregon, the strength of the "Salem Clique" had weakened perceptibly. In an early caucus held that year, the party split into two factions. Those who broke away were critical of the "Salem Clique," and some, in addition, were outspoken in their support of slavery. The regular party was able to maintain control despite these defections, and in a later caucus held to elect delegates to the constitutional convention the following resolution was offered and approved:

> That each member of the Democratic party in Oregon may freely speak and act according to his individual convictions of right and policy upon the question of slavery in Oregon, without in any manner impairing his standing in the Democratic party on that account-provided that nothing in these resolutions shall be construed in toleration of black republicanism, abolition, or any other factor or organization arrayed in opposition to the Democratic party.[9]

The second political party, the Whigs, offered a weak challenge to the Democrats. Traditionally the party of aristocracy and wealth, it had few advocates in Oregon. It was loosely organized and differed little in point of view from the Democratic party. It supported the peculiar interpretation of popular sovereignty favored by most Oregonians, but on the question of slavery deferred to the authority of the federal government. Failure to offer a strong party platform opposing slavery prompted anti-slavery Whigs to organize independent of the party.

In June 1855, an anti-slavery convention was held in Albany. Attended by Whigs, members of the clergy, and other citizens opposed to slavery, the convention adopted eight resolutions condemning the Fugitive Slave Act, the repeal of the Missouri Compromise, and vowed to fight any attempt to introduce slavery into Oregon. A program was prepared to initiate the campaign: county meetings were proposed to bring public attention to the evils of slavery, and the election of anti-slavery candidates and the publication of anti-slavery newspapers was supported. A meeting was planned for the following October to prepare a formal platform.

In May 1856, a group of Jackson County residents opposed to slavery met to create a Republican party organization. Their platform called on the federal government to prohibit slavery in the territories, but another resolution affirmed the right of the local populace to elect their public officials. Clearly, it was an attempt to redefine the doctrine of popular sovereignty in terms that would appeal to Oregonians, without taking a stand on the issue of slavery. Other political organizations opposed to slavery met, also calling themselves Republicans. Sensitive to critics that called them radicals, these

Republicans modified their position on slavery, opposing it in Oregon but favoring non-interference in areas where it already existed.

In spite of the infant party's retreat from strong anti-slavery statements, Republicans were labeled as abolitionists and often called "Black Republicans," and most Oregonians were at first unwilling to join this party, regardless of their personal convictions on slavery in Oregon. In 1856, David Logan, a pioneer attorney, commented,

> . . . the Whigs are all dead out here—they call themselves the Republican party—which means negro worshippers . . . I'll see the Republicans to the devil before I'll vote with them. I don't know what I am exactly, but anything but an abolitionist.[10]

In the early years of the 1850s, the issue of slavery was the subject of an occasional article in the local newspapers. These were characteristically either attacks on the eastern abolitionist movement, or theoretical discussions of the evils of slavery. In 1851, the *Oregon Statesman* reprinted an article published in the Richmond, Virginia *Examiner,* "by request." Spread over four columns of a seven column page, the article condemned abolitionists who were working for civil rights for black people.

> Their assertions that Negroes are entitled to approach our polls, to sit in our courts, to places in our Legislature are not more rational than a demand upon them that they let all adult bulls vote at their polls, all capable goats enjoy a chance at their ermine, all asses (quadruped) the privilege of running for their General Assemblies and all swine for their seats in Congress.[11]

The same year, the *Oregon Spectator* published a lengthy letter from a local reader, predicting that Oregon would very soon become a state, and that the people would have to decide on several issues, the most important being slavery.

> I am opposed to the principle of slavery, and in this enlightened age of civilization, and more especially in a government, like ours, whose boast is its republican principles, and its free institutions, to hold in bondage (and that perpetual) a part of the race of man, is revolting in the extreme.[12]

The author went on to say that those opposed to slavery had been able to do nothing more than keep the issue alive in the press. He maintained that anyone who sought to prevent the migration of black settlers to free states in the West was as guilty of prejudice as those who supported slavery.

> If men feel so much for the race, let them endeavor to make their condition better and not endeavor to pen them up in stalls like brutes.[13]

He concluded by proposing that those who talked about freeing slaves should buy one, bring him to Oregon and give him his freedom.

> . . . not until then can the sectarian, the philanthropist, and the man that boasts of his charity say that he has done all that he could, to relieve suffering humanity.[14]

When slavery became possible if not likely in Oregon after the passage of the Kansas-Nebraska Act in 1854, the slavery issue in the press took on a more distinctly local character. Articles were often the products of rival editors engaged in political and personal warfare. The *Oregon Statesman* was particularly vicious in condemning outspoken anti-slavery groups, which it called "abolitionist" whether or not these groups actually advocated the total prohibition of slavery in the United States. After the anti-slavery convention held in Albany in 1855, the *Oregon Statesman* called the delegates "old grannies," and "nigger-struck dames," and refused to publish the resolutions passed by the convention. The editor concluded, "If anything could make the people of Oregon desire slavery, it would be the agitation of the subject by such fanatics as these."[15] A letter from Delazon Smith, who claimed to have attended the convention, was also published.

> In my humble judgement there is about as much danger –about as fair a possibility of slavery's going to the moon . . . as there is of its being precipitated upon *our* Territory. There can be no reasonable question but that at this moment, nineteen-twentieths of the people of Oregon, would, if called upon to decide the question at the ballot box, vote *against* establishing slavery here.[16]

Smith declared that there were no slaves within 3,000 miles of Oregon, and that there was no disposition among Oregonians to own them. He concluded by warning that if slavery were introduced, it would be as a reaction to the abolitionists.

Thomas Dryer, editor of the Portland *Weekly Oregonian,* was a Whig and a member of the Territorial Assembly. The leading public critic of the

Democratic party, he also resented the emerging Republican party, because it had adopted many of the political views of the Whigs. In July 1856, he published an editorial critical of national events over slavery and the political motivations of the pro-slavery elements which threatened to destroy the Union.

> It appears that madness has seized hold of the advocates and defenders of slavery, and that the utmost recklessness has taken possession of those men in authority to *over-awe* and *crush out* the right of the citizen to think for himself. In connexion with this slavery question, all law, all precedent, justice and humanity are competely disregarded and violated. When the end of this will be, no man can tell.[17]

In another editorial published the same year, Dryer attacked Joseph Lane's involvement with the pro-slavery advocates in Washington, D.C., and asserted that Lane, who had been elected as Oregon's representative to Congress after the death of Samuel Thurston, did not represent the interests of the majority of Oregonians, but only a small group who sought political office. He said Lane's sympathy for slavery could mean only one thing: that the party that supported him in Oregon was beginning to support the idea of slavery in Oregon. Dryer disavowed any sympathy with abolitionists, but said,

> We are opposed to the extension of slavery over free territory within the boundaries of the United States, unless the people desire it.[18]

Referring to Delazon Smith's resolutions to support the repeal of the Missouri Compromise and the passage of the Kansas-Nebraska Act, Dryer said,

> This was done for the purpose of bringing the party up to the work of making Oregon a *slave state,* whenever it would conduce to the interests or advancement of the leaders of the so-called democracy.[19]

Dryer continued to denounce the "Salem Clique," and accused them of making slavery an issue of party obedience.

> They are, however, to rule under new issues and by a new process. We must have slavery here, say they; we must tell them that labor is entirely too high, and that every democrat must go in for slavery in Oregon as a democratic measure.[20]

As if thoroughly sick of the issue, he concluded:

> Let us have a state government and make the issue at once. If we are to have slavery forced upon us, let it be by the people here and not by the slavery propagandists at Washington City. If the majority of the people in Oregon, fairly expressed, desire slavery, we are too much of a democrat to further oppose introduction.[21]

Thomas Dryer continued to criticize the Democratic party, commented on the appearance of pro-slavery newspapers, criticized outspoken supporters of slavery and urged his readers to decide on the issue independent of party affiliation. His editorial tone was frequently shrill and repetitive; as a representative of the minority political party he spent a good deal of energy engaged in private warfare with the Democrats. Dryer's small press had sat on the Portland dock for months, delaying the first issue of the newspaper, where he complained that Captain Hall of the Navigation Company had said he didn't care when he delivered the freight for the "little damn Whig paper in Portland."[22]

In spite of the invective that passed between Dryer and Bush, their position regarding slavery was similar. Both were motivated strictly by local self-interests rather than high moral or ethical ideals. Neither supported the introduction of slavery into Oregon; both sought to appeal to their readers and gain support for their own political party.

Most of the avid supporters of slavery were Democrats, and Bush pacified them by a strong condemnation of anti-slavery agitators. His opposition to slavery was based on economic considerations. In March 1857, he predicted that the voters would not be influenced by moral or judicial considerations, but would vote in terms of the economic advantages or disadvantages of slavery. He admitted that Oregon would probably come into the Union as a free state, but warned again that if abolitionists flocked to Oregon the citizens would react by supporting slavery. He stated:

> We have no slaves here. A very few blacks who were slaves in the states have been brought by their owners, but they have understood they were free. The courts, when appealed to, have declared them free, by virtue of the act of Congress. We have but few free niggers here, but quite as many of that class as we wish ever to see.[23]

In a later editorial Bush expressed the desire to see constitutional provisions which would exclude black people from Oregon, and make it a crime for any white person to bring blacks into the state. In addition, he suggested that laws be passed which would prevent them from buying real estate, bringing a suit in court, or enforcing any contracts or agreements. Black people should not be allowed to become citizens in any real sense, he believed, and would be placed under such disadvantages as would tend to discourage them from trying to come to Oregon.

> With these restrictions, disabilities and consequent prohibition of negroes and mulattoes, we are for a free state in Oregon . . . In arriving at this conclusion we are not influenced by hostility to the institution of African slavery *per se*. We are of the opinion that in the sugar and cotton growing states it is a necessary, if not undispensible system of labor. We believe, also that the African, whatever his "nominal" condition, is destined to be the servant and subordinate of the superior white race and that it is best for both races that the servitude and subordination should be regulated by law. And we believe, also that the wisdom of man has not yet devised a system under which the negro is as well off as he is under that of American slavery. Still we think that our climate, soil, situation, population, etc., render [it] to any useful extent an "impossible" institution for Oregon.[24]

Bush encouraged his readers to contribute letters on slavery which he printed, as well as editorials from other newspapers which expressed his philosophy. One citizen, F. S. Martin, argued in favor of slavery in a letter published in August 1857. Martin stated that slaves would thrive in Oregon's mild climate and that crops could be easily harvested by them. He predicted that Oregon could not reach its agricultural potential without slave labor, and that the population would quickly double if they were introduced.

Other letters published during 1857 opposed or favored slavery on economic grounds. Those opposed feared that the state would be flooded with abolitionists if slavery were introduced, and the close proximity of free areas would make it difficult to retrieve slaves if they ran away. Some opposed slavery because it would create a slave owning aristocracy, reminiscent of the "poor white" fears expressed by Jesse Applegate. One correspondent wrote,

> I see no reason why the scarcity of women in Oregon should cause us to bring here the withering blighting curse of slavery—to create style and establish an aristocratic spirit in our midst—to cause the rich man with his slaves to lord it over his poor neighbor—to see our sons working side by side with the rich man's slave.[25]

Politics in the early months of 1857 had become a confusing spectacle of rival factions intent on breaking the stranglehold of the Salem Clique, thought to be in control of the majority of Oregonians, still silent on the issue of slavery. But when the Supreme Court handed down its decision in the case of *Dred Scott* v. *Sanford,* declaring that only a sovereign state could legally prohibit slavery, one thing became clear. Oregon must vote for statehood, and soon if slavery was to be avoided. The process for calling a convention was conducted with amazing speed, and without the consent of the federal government. Application for statehood was approved in June 1857, and delegates convened in August to write the constitution. By the time of the constitutional convention, the slavery issue had substantially eroded the power of the "Salem Clique," and one-third of the delegates were independent of its control.

4

Within Every Rule

Legislation in Oregon 1857–1860

In June of 1857 the voters of Oregon approved the question of statehood by a vote of 7,617 to 1,679. It was approved in every county except Wasco, which took in all the area east of the Cascades. Previous elections on the question of statehood—in 1854, 1855 and 1856—had been defeated.[1] The statehood issue was first supported by the Democratic party; Whigs and Republicans were in the minority and opposed statehood because they would not participate in political appointments or receive any other political benefits. Without some distinct advantage, voters were reluctant to approve the increase in taxation that would come with statehood.

The decisive shift in public opinion in 1857 can be traced to several events. James Buchanan was inaugurated president in March, 1857, after defeating the Republican presidential candidate, John C. Fremont. Buchanan's record on slavery was disturbing to citizens of Oregon: he had opposed the Wilmot Proviso, supported the Compromise of 1850 which maintained the balance between slave and free states, and in 1857 attempted to force Kansas to accept the Lecompton Constitution, which would have permitted slavery there. Oregonians looked at "bloody Kansas" and feared that slavery might be forced upon them in the same way.

The Supreme Court decision in the Dred Scott case, in March of 1857, added fuel to their fears. The decision nullified the Missouri Compromise and struck down any federal or territorial law that prevented slaveowners from owning slaves or from taking them anywhere within the borders of the United States. Only sovereign states, said the court, could permit or forbid slavery.

In the summer of 1857, on the eve of the constitutional convention, the *Oregon Statesman* published a lengthy discussion of the slavery issue called a "Free State Letter," written by George H. Williams, the judge who, five years earlier, awarded custody of the Holmes children to their parents.

Williams argued for the admission of Oregon as a free state. In doing so, he admitted opposing his pro-slavery friends. He began by reviewing the historical decisions which had excluded slavery from Oregon, and favored a continuance of that policy. Admitting that he did not oppose slavery where it already existed, he pointed out that Thomas Jefferson, a slaveowner, had supported the Ordinance of 1787, which banned slavery in the Northwest Territory. He gave several examples where slavery had been on the decline in the South because of economic conditions until abolitionists interfered and brought the issue into the political arena. Indiana, like Oregon, had experienced a labor shortage and petitioned Congress to allow slavery. The petition was denied because it was not in the best economic interest of the nation to allow slavery in a northern state.

Williams next introduced a lengthy argument designed to prove that slavery was undesirable in Oregon from an economic point of view. Slave labor was involuntary, he said, and Oregon was settled and improved by those who stood to gain from their own efforts. Slaves were lazy and would work only to avoid punishment. They would be idled during the rainy winter season and might easily escape to California or Canada. Fugitive slaves might join with Indians against whites, he said, echoing earlier arguments in support of exclusion laws. The presence of free black people would degrade the labor market, and whites who were unwilling to work as domestics or field hands would move elsewhere. Williams also feared the political consequences of voting for slavery as the South did not demand it, and the North would strongly oppose it.

> Can Oregon, with her great claims, present and prospective, upon the government, afford to throw away the friendship of the North—the overruling power of the nation—for the sake of slavery?[2]

He urged the people of Oregon to consult their own best interests and vote for a free state. While disclaiming any sympathy for abolitionists, he maintained that the federal government had no power to decide the issue for the people of Oregon, and denied that Democrats had to support slavery out of party loyalty.

Williams later commented on this letter and the slavery debates of 1857. Many of the Democrats who supported slavery, he maintained, were from the border states of the Midwest and held large claims of land which they were finding difficult to cultivate alone. Under the apprehension that their arguments would convince the majority to support slavery, he wrote the letter.

In August 1857, in a year of intense debate over slavery, delegates met in Salem to write the state constitution. The convention elected as its president Matthew Deady, the only delegate to run on a pro-slavery ticket. Of the sixty delegates, thirty-one were farmers. The rest were lawyers, miners, newspaper writers, one civil engineer, and three territorial judges. Information given about the delegates' last state of residence before moving to Oregon reveals that forty-seven of the sixty delegates had lived in Ohio, Indiana, Illinois, Michigan, Iowa, or Missouri. Many were probably familiar with exclusion laws or constitutional exclusion clauses considered in Illinois, Indiana, and Iowa.[3]

Thomas Dryer, a delegate, published an editorial shortly after the convention opened complaining bitterly about the leadership that was emerging, the election of Deady as president, and the solidarity the Democrats were displaying in support of the "Salem Clique." Even George Williams, suffering from criticism in the aftermath of the publication of his "Free State Letter," had come crawling back to the fold. "Freedom and slavery," Dryer declared, "are apparently the only questions which excite the least interest or are talked about."[4]

Matthew Deady appointed nine delegates to a committee authorized to prepare the schedule of issues to be submitted to the voters, which included the approval of the constitution and the dual questions of slavery and an exclusion clause. All questions concerning slavery were to be referred to this committee and not discussed on the floor of the convention. The majority of the members of this committee held pro-slavery views.[5] After these opening maneuvers, the slavery issue was dropped. Only Jesse Applegate, fearing that debates over slavery would dominate the convention, introduced a resolution declaring all debate on slavery out of order. This resolution was defeated and the delegates proceeded to draft the constitution, relying for guidance on the constitutions of midwestern states, particularly Indiana, Iowa, and Michigan.

Contrary to prediction, slavery was not again debated, but the status of black people was discussed as clauses were proposed. The right to vote was restricted to white men only and specifically denied to black men. After some debate, Chinese were excluded as well. An attempt was made to limit public schools to white children only, but was defeated because it would exclude half-breed children.

An exclusion clause to be inserted into the Bill of Rights, if approved by the voters, was debated, and an unsuccessful effort was made to strike it from the ballot. Some delegates wanted to include Chinese in the exclusion clause, and the relative merits of blacks and Chinese as laborers were debated. Some delegates felt that Chinese made better domestic servants, while others said they were a great evil in the mines. George Williams argued that Oregon should be reserved for white people, while Thomas Dryer said he "would vote to exclude Negroes, Chinamen, Kanakas, and even Indians. The association of these races with the white was the demoralization of the latter."[6]

The constitution was adopted by the delegates in September, but the vote was not unanimous. Ten voted against adoption, and fifteen others were absent, including Jesse Applegate, who had left the convention in disgust. In a letter to Matthew Deady he wrote,

> . . . the free Negro section is perfectly abominable, and it is hard to realize that men having hearts and consciences, some of them today in the front ranks of the defenders of human rights, could be led so far by party prejudice as to put such an article in the frame of a government intended to be free and just.[7]

During the debate preceding the vote to adopt, Thomas Dryer and William Watkins expressed their disappointment with the way the slavery and exclusion questions had been handled. Dryer, predictably, complained that the Democrats had prevented free state delegates from voicing their opinions and that the convention had shirked its duty by failing to debate the slavery issue. William Watkins objected to the exclusion clause, particularly a section that denied black people the right to bring a suit in court. Denying that he was an abolitionist, he said that he did not feel obliged to treat black people as his equals. Still, under this clause they would have no legal protections at all.

> Under this barbarous provision (for I can use no milder term) the negro is cast upon the world with no defense; his life, liberty, his property, his all, are dependent on the caprice, the passion, and the inveterate prejudices of not only the community at large but of every felon who may happen to cover an inhuman heart with a white face.[8]

If there was any way to prevent black people from coming to Oregon without denying them justice he would favor such a bill, but he could not support legislation that would place other human beings so completely outside the protection of the law.

In November 1857, the voters approved the constitution by a vote of 7,195 to 3,215. Slavery was defeated by a vote of 2,65 yes to 7,727 no. The exclusion clause, which on the ballot read "Do you vote for free Negroes in

Oregon? Yes, or No," received the highest number of favorable votes, 8,640 voting for exclusion, 1,081 against.[9]

The margin of defeat on the slavery issue suggests that the slavery controversy was more apparent than real. One Democrat remarked, "There was not much agitation."[10] Another observer recalled,

> . . . [that was] the situation in Oregon at that time, whose people were in far more danger of the introduction of slavery among them than the people of Kansas were at any time. True, they were not harassed by any border ruffian invasion or any flagrant interference of the Washington administration, but their apathy or rather their slavish subservience to party discipline was truly appalling.[11]

The political waters were indeed muddy on the issue of slavery. While the Democratic party included factions which supported or opposed slavery, their planned program of silence amounted to a studied indifference on the issue. The Whigs and Republicans did not fare much better. Determined to support the peculiar interpretation of popular sovereignty which guaranteed local self control, they nevertheless chose not to address the issue of slavery except by saying that it should be solved by the federal government.

The slavery issue in the press was frequently personal and partisan if also characterized by a brilliant mastery of invective prose that has come to be called the "Oregon style" of journalism. The *Weekly Oregonian* and *Oregon Argus* had limited circulation, and probably were not read by one-eighth of the population. The *Oregonian* has been called "a distinctively Whig journal with incidental anti-slavery proclivities."[12] W. L. Adams, editor of the *Oregon Argus,* was called "the chief informer, energizer and rally center of the distinctively anti-slavery forces of that day."[13] In October 1857, between the adoption of the constitution by the delegates and the public vote, the *Oregon Argus* published a letter critical of the exclusion clause.

> Now in the name of justice and humanity, what induced the Convention to say anything about free negroes? Are we overrun with them, or are we likely to be? Are they more troublesome than Indians? . . . Shall we, men of the nineteenth century, surrounded by the lights of civilization, by the arts and sciences, by the onward strides of freedom, and by the bright and softening rays of revelation, shall we, I say, support a Constitution which provides that human slavery, intolerance, persecution and tyranny, may under any circumstances be made the rule of government?[14]

The *Oregon Statesman* was widely read, and had great influence among

Democrats. Although Bush by reputation supported a free state, his casual contempt for outspoken critics of slavery and his position within the "Salem Clique" and close personal identity with Southerners such as Joseph Lane, fueled the fears of the opponents of slavery.

It was characteristic for advocates of a free state to preface their arguments by disavowing any sympathy with abolitionists, and evidence suggests that the most effective argument was the strictly practical economic analysis of slavery presented in Williams' "Free State Letter." One observer of the era noted the effect this letter had on public opinion.

> After the circulation of this address, any observing person could notice that a change was taking place; any sensitive person could feel it. The people for whom the address was intended were beginning to discover themselves and think aloud. And I assert that what is here written is no afterthought, but the results of inquiry and observation made at the time.[15]

Some people, this writer asserted, who had intended to support slavery changed their minds as a result of this letter.

> At Roseburg, the home of General Lane and Judge M. P. Deady, whose influence, whether authorized or not was in favor of the institution, I learned from a Reverend Anderson that the tide had turned, and that he met with surprises every day. In Rogue River Valley I was assured by my cousins that the tide was running out quite rapidly. The noisy slaveocrats of Jackson County had been claiming that county for slavery, but many people were exercising their fancy in supposing the consequences that might ensue when runaway niggers should get with the Modoc and Klamath Indians. The picture was not agreeable. The people of southern Oregon had had enough of Indian warfare. The aforementioned impediments to slavery extension as well as others, were brought to the front by the Judge, in plain, straightforward and forcible language, which no doubt set the people to thinking more connectedly and comprehensively than they otherwise would; and while the effects of such a lesson in ratiocination may not be estimated with any approach to accuracy, I am confident that it was the most timely and the most effective appeal published during the whole of the controversy.[16]

Faced with a decision, Oregonians were not aided by party rhetoric or yellow journalism, but by a single letter which appealed not to their moral conscience, but to their economic self-interest. That, apparently, was enough.

The admission of Oregon by Congress was not without opposition and delay; congressional debate was dominated by political and sectional considerations. As early as 1854, Joseph Lane had urged Congress to pass an act authorizing the formation of a state government in Oregon, but the bill introduced that year and another introduced in 1856 were defeated. Oregon thus formed its constitution without formal authorization by the federal government.

The main opposition to statehood had come from southern Congressmen, who feared that the admission of Oregon would upset the balance between slave and free states. Once Congress had an opportunity to examine the constitution, objections were raised by northern Congressmen as well. Several Senators expressed dismay over the exclusion clause. Senator Wilson of Massachusetts, for example, regretted that he could not approve the admission of Oregon, but said that its constitution contained provisions that were "inhuman and unchristian."[17] He admitted that black people in Massachusetts had not attained full social equality, but believed that they were accorded full rights as citizens under the law. He defended the character of black people and their participation in the Revolutionary War, observing that the rights of Massachusetts black people would be severely restricted should they ever visit Oregon.

> If the descendants of those brave men should go on board a whale ship, go to the Pacific Ocean, land in Oregon, in stress of weather, it may be, go on shore, be smitten down, nearly murdered, by white villains, without cause, they cannot maintain a suit in the courts of that State. They may be abused, they may be murdered, any outrage may be inflicted, any indignity may be put upon them, but they cannot maintain a suit in the Courts of that State to protect them in their personal rights. Is this not inhuman, unchristian, devilish? I cannot vote to sanction a proposition which outlaws men for no crime.[18]

Senators opposed to the exclusion clause believed that Congress had the power to admit or deny admission to any state because of discriminatory laws (although they could not censure a state already admitted for the same reason).

Many Senators, however, defended the constitution, saying that Oregonians had every right to exclude black people if they wished to do so. They pointed out the ordered way in which it had been written, while Kansas was involved in a bitter struggle for admission with a constitution that proposed to protect slaveowners and exclude free black people. One Senator argued:

> Oregon is within every rule that has been laid down to justify the admission of Kansas under the Lecompton Constitution, and, at the same time, she has avoided every objection that has been urged as a insuperable one to the admission of Kansas.[19]

The bill to admit Oregon was passed in the Senate in May 1858. Once again it was referred to the House, and later that year became involved in a partisan struggle. Some members of the House repeated objections to the exclusion clause, but the partisan contest was essentially between Republicans favoring the admission of Kansas, and Democrats the admission of Oregon. The final vote in the House reflected these alignments: three-fifths of the southern vote, all Democrats, favored admission, while over four-fifths of the Republicans voted against it. The final vote was 114 in favor, 103 opposed. President Buchanan signed the bill two days later, and on February 14, 1859, Oregon became a state. It holds the distinction of being the only free state admitted to the Union with an exclusion clause in its constitution. It was a clear victory for settlers who came to the Far West to escape the racial troubles of the East. Oregon was to remain a remote Eden, dedicated to the destinies of white men only.

Between the writing of the Constitution and formal admission to the Union, the territorial legislature continued to meet and, in 1857, bills to protect slave property were proposed, indicating that the laws in Oregon banning slavery were not always observed.

Some evidence of slavery can be found in court cases and legal records of transfers of property. The most famous court case concerned the Holmes children. In the early 1850s Joseph Teal purchased a black boy and his grandmother from a man named Southworth, who lived in Lane County. Teal freed the pair, and they settled on the Long Tom River near Junction City[a]. A black woman, Luteshia Censor[b], sued the estate of her former owner for wages she had earned while living in Oregon.[20] Other less formal

a There is uncertainty about this. Sources conflict on the date of this alleged transaction, and the deed of sale said to have been drawn up by Judge Riley Stratton has not been located. The author's sources state the boy went by the name "Cole" and that he and his grandmother were sold to Teal by James Southworth soon after reaching Oregon. In the 1860 census, an eight-year-old Black child named "Cole Southwell" was listed in the Lane County residence of Thomas Driskill. The Driskills lived in Elmira, not far from the Southwell family; however, there is no relation between the Southworths and the Southwells. In the 1880 census, Cole, now known as "William Coleman" was working as a cook in Eugene. He died in Lane County in 1899.

b Letitia Carson was a Black woman who lived for seven years in Benton County with David Carson, a white man, with whom she had two children. After David's death in 1852, Letitia was unable to be named as his survivor and their shared home and property was sold away in a probate auction by a neighbor named Greenberry Smith, who had been appointed executor of David's estate. Letitia successfully sued Smith for compensation by claiming she was due back wages for her years of service to David. See Bob Zybach, "Strangely Absent from History: Carson vs. Smith, 1852–1856," *Oregon State Bar Bulletin* (2016).

arrangements existed between whites and blacks who came to Oregon together, but in 1857 it became clear that some slaves were being held in Oregon in the same sense as slaves were held in other areas of the country.

The Legislative Assembly of 1857, uncertain of its authority, accomplished little. As if to illustrate the frivolity of the session, Thomas Dryer, writing shortly before the session ended, concluded by remarking that the leading subject of attention seemed to be granting petitions of divorce. "There seems to be a wonderful amount of matrimonial unhappiness in Oregon…"[21]

The government was in limbo. Still bound by territorial law, it awaited admission to the Union under a free constitution. The Dred Scott decision had denied the power of a territory to legislate against slaveowners, and thus, barely two months after voters had rejected slavery, bills to protect slave property were proposed. William Allen, a Democrat from Yamhill County, introduced the resolution.

> . . . it has been decided by the Supreme Court of the United States, that Congress has no power to prohibit the introduction of slavery into the Territory . . . slavery *is* tolerated by the Constitution of the United States; Therefore, Resolved, That the Chair appoint a committee of three, to report what legislation is necessary to protect the rights of persons holding slaves in this Territory.[22]

He then commented:

> . . . I don't see any reason why we should not have laws protecting slavery. There are slaves here, but no laws to regulate or protect this kind of property.[23]

Debate against the Allen resolution was led by Thomas Dryer, who reminded the Assembly that the voters of Oregon had just banned slavery. The majority were opposed to the resolution, and it was easily defeated, but during the course of debate several members admitted that they knew people who owned slaves. J. W. Mack said that one of his neighbors in Lane County owned slaves, and was in California trying to test the validity of the Fugitive Slave Law to recover some of his runaway slaves. Mack argued in favor of the resolution, in spite of the vote that had just been taken.

> It makes no difference whether the constitution prohibits slavery or not, the fact is there are men here who own property in slaves. Are they to be protected in that property? I have no idea but this legislation will be lost the very day after the constitution takes effect, but slaveowners

have a right to ask protection till then.[24]

Another member said that although he had voted for a free state, Oregon was still a territory and should pass laws protecting slaveowners, and also slaves. He predicted, "In all probability before another year shall roll around, we shall have double the number of slaves we have here now. Why not give them some protection?"[25]

The resolution was indefinitely postponed, but Allen, not satisfied, introduced another resolution near the end of the session. When Thomas Dryer objected, saying that slavery did not exist in Oregon, Allen responded:

> The gentleman says that slavery does not exist here. Well, it has been proved, upon this floor that slavery does exist in this Territory in several counties. There are some in Benton, Lane, Polk, Yamhill, and I know not how many other counties. That matter was fairly proved on this floor on a former occasion, and I do not deem it necessary to bring any other proof than the veracity of honorable gentlemen who are representatives of their constituents here . . . Well, sir, slavery property is here! It then becomes our duty to protect that property as recognized by the constitution of the United States.[26]

After listening to a long speech in opposition to the resolution, Allen withdrew it, as defeat was certain.

Between the introduction of the two resolutions, Allen presented a petition from M. R. Crisp and forty-six other citizens, asking the legislators to pass a law protecting slave property. Two days later, Allen offered a lengthy bill in response to the petition. Nine sections were devoted to procedures by which runaway slaves were to be apprehended and returned to their owners. Fines were to be levied against anyone aiding a runaway slave, to compensate for the economic loss to their owner. Any master convicted of mistreating a slave would be fined twenty dollars. The bill was defeated by a vote of fifteen to seven.

Oregon's constitution provided for an election to be held on the first Monday of June to elect the first state officials, and although Oregon was not yet formally admitted to the Union, these elections were held in 1858. The Democratic party was successful in securing the election of its party nominees for Congress and state governor, and seated a majority in the state legislature. Oregonians, who had the previous year banned slavery, now elected as governor John Whiteaker and as congressional representative Lafayette Grover, both of whom were outspoken in their support of slavery.

The state legislature was scheduled to meet in the autumn of 1858, but its members, realizing that they had no legal authority, deferred to the members of the territorial assembly and the last session was convened in December. The question of slave property was again considered, prompted by four petitions presented on behalf of slave-owning citizens of Oregon. Another slave protection bill was drafted, and eventually defeated. The assembly was uncertain of its legal authority and reluctant to pass laws which might outrage national public sentiment.

The paradox that existed in Oregon politics in the late 1850s, demonstrated in the contradictory votes to prohibit slavery, support laws that would protect slaveowners, and elect a pro-slavery governor and representative to Congress, was not without a recent precedent on the West Coast. Californians had also elected slavery sympathizers, William H. Gwin and John B. Weller, to deliver its free state constitution to Congress. One observer accounted for the inconsistency in California by explaining the motivations of the voters.

> From mere selfishness, they could not brook slavery within their own borders, but they wanted to be citizens of a State and sovereign over their own local affairs, and knowing that slavery was dominant in the general government, they must present as few points of antagonism as possible to the powers that be, so that their prayer for admission might be speedily realized. Besides, they wanted appropriations for their harbors and rivers and coast defenses, and none of these were likely to be answered when presented by men opposed to their system.[27]

Oregonians were unwilling to censure their leaders simply because they held pro-slavery views. Possibly they did not care. They were also motivated by personal and economic considerations. Even some free-state Democrats had been known to say, "I shall vote against slavery, but if it carries I shall get me a nigger."[28] The repeated introduction of bills to protect slave property is indicative of the existence of a die-hard pro-slavery faction in Oregon that refused to admit defeat.

5

No Farther into the Dark Clouds

Legislation in Oregon 1860–1875

In 1860 the black population of Oregon according to the census was 128. Many of these individuals were living independent of white families, working as farmers, miners, shingle makers, washerwomen, barbers, cooks, blacksmiths and common laborers. A number of them still lived with white families as domestic servants, and a few were listed as slaves. An early black resident of Portland, A.E. Flowers, described conditions in the decade of the 1860s.

> When I arrived in Portland there was only one Negro church in the whole town, the "People's Church" which was an independent organization. It was organized in 1862. At this time colored people were not allowed to own any property. They were not allowed to go into any kind of business and they were not allowed to vote. Every Negro had to pay a $10.00 head tax. The colored people had no civil rights. It was very difficult to get jobs except as a menial.[1]

The politics of that decade did not ease difficulties for black people: a poll tax, ban on intermarriage, threats of enforcing the exclusion clause, a reluctant support for the North during the Civil War, and the failure of the legislature to ratify all the federal constitutional amendments placed restrictions on the freedom and spirit of the few black people who lived in Oregon.

The national election of 1860 was fought over the issue raised by the Dred Scott decision: the extension or prohibition of slavery in the territories. The split in the national Democratic party was widening, brought on by increasing opposition to slavery and growing resentment against the southern Democrats' insistence on caucus sovereignty. The pro-slavery Democrats left the convention of 1860 and met separately, nominating as their presidential candidate John C. Breckinridge. When the Oregon and California delegates followed, Joseph Lane of Oregon became the vice-presidential candidate. The northern wing of the Democratic party nominated Stephen O. Douglas, and the Republican convention nominated Abraham Lincoln.

The split within Oregon's Democratic party was widening, brought on by internal opposition to the pro-slavery faction headed by Lane and Delazon Smith. George H. Williams began to canvass the state, running for the U.S. Senate. Later, he recalled his reasons for opposing Smith.

> The agitation of the slavery question had now reached a crisis. The good Lord and good devil style of politics had now become disgusting. I made up my mind that, as far as my opportunities allowed, I would resist the further aggression of the slave power and oppose the election to office of those who favored it. Accordingly, in the month of March, 1860, I went into Linn County, to the residence of Delazon Smith, and said to him: "Delazon, I have come to beard the lion in his den (Smith's friends called him the 'Lion of Linn'); I am going to canvass Linn County, and my object is to beat you and General Lane for the Senate. Come on and make your fight."[2]

The majority of Oregonians saw the danger of secession implied by the Breckinridge/Lane ticket and elected James W. Nesmith, a Douglas Democrat, and Edward D. Baker, Republican, to represent Oregon in the U.S. Senate.

In spite of a coalition forming between Douglas Democrats and Republicans, the legislature of 1860 was still controlled by the regular Democratic party. Again, the exclusion of black people was proposed, prompted in part by petitions and also by the need to pass legislation to enforce the exclusion clause of the state constitution. The first bill, offered in the Senate, penalized anyone bringing a black person, slave or free, into Oregon. The fines were between $500 and $1,000; failure to pay the fine would mean a prison sentence. The penalty for black people who came on their own was a $50 fine or two months hard labor. The crime for blacks was a misdemeanor; a jury trial and appeal rights were guaranteed. The higher penalties imposed on people who brought blacks to Oregon suggests that the bill was primarily intended to discourage slaveowners from bringing slaves to Oregon.

The House bill was prompted by two petitions. One, presented by 293 citizens of Multnomah County, complained that black and Chinese people were becoming an intolerable nuisance in that part of the state, crowding in and taking over jobs that poor whites had held.

> They are of no benefit to the State either socially, morally or politically—they pay no taxes, and the Chinamen after accumulating large amounts of money carry it to the celestial land. We therefore ask your [honorable] bodies to provide by law for the removal of the negroes and such provisions in reference to Chinamen as to cause them to prefer some other country to ours.[3]

This bill proposed that the fine for bringing blacks into the state would be $200, and $10 for blacks who had come themselves. The presiding judge could extend the time a black person had before he must leave. Neither bill passed.

> In Oregon, as well as elsewhere, 1861 was a year of excitement. The war and anti-war feeling was at fever heat. Every hill and valley found a tongue, and firey speeches were made for and against the government.[4]

The Civil War had begun when Oregonians were preoccupied in efforts to subdue the Indian tribes. Although the Indian wars had officially ended in 1858, a group of white people was attacked by Indians in September 1860 near Fort Hall. Of forty-four, only fifteen survived. The legislature requested that the federal government send more troops to fight the Indians, but as the conflict in the East grew, troops already in Oregon were transferred, leaving fewer than 700 by the spring of 1861.

In May 1861, little more than a month after the firing on Fort Sumter, Governor Whiteaker, whose southern sentiments were well-known, advised the people of Oregon not to become involved in the war, which he characterized as a "domestic disorder."[5] Although settlers had come from both North and South, he maintained that peace and tranquility existed in Oregon. He said Union party meetings being held throughout the state were creating disorder, and maintained that those opposed to the war were not disloyal. Predicting that the war would easily be won by the North without any help from Oregon, he said Oregonians should concentrate on protecting the frontier from Indian attacks. Whiteaker said further that the North would never be able to re-establish friendly relations with the South, and that the freeing of the slaves, like the freeing of the slaves in the Roman Empire, would sow the seeds of its own destruction. He warned the North to protect its institutions, saying, "Have a care that in freeing the Negro you do not enslave the white man."[6]

The opening of the Civil War prompted a realignment of political parties in Oregon. The Whig party, by now virtually non-existent, had merged with the Republicans. Free State Democrats were unwilling to identify with this party, still under the stigma "Black Republican," but in 1861 the party name was dropped and citizens were invited to unite under the name of the Union party. The coalition that resulted succeeded in defeating the regular Democratic party and in 1862 the Union party seated a majority in the state legislature.

In spite of a shift in power away from the pro-slavery Democrats, this legislative session passed two bills that discriminated against black people. The first was an annual poll tax of five dollars to be paid by "every Negro, Chinaman, [Hawaiian] and Mulatto residing within the limits of this state."[7] The local sheriff was responsible for collecting the tax. If it could not be paid, it could be worked out on the public roads at 50¢ a day. This bill was accidentally repealed in 1864 and attempts to revive it in 1866 failed.[8] The second law passed in this session prohibited marriages between whites and persons of one-fourth or more Negro blood. A code of civil procedure approved in 1862 made no mention of race, and allowed black people to be witnesses in the courts of the state, although they could not act as jurors. The right of black children to attend public school was affirmed in the Codes and Laws of 1862 which held that schools should be "free to all persons between the age of four and twenty years."[9]

The legislative session of 1864, still controlled by the Union party, considered a bill requiring that a census of all black people in each county be taken to determine how many were living in Oregon illegally under the terms of the exclusion clause. The local sheriff was empowered to take the census, issue warrants, and deport all blacks without any intervening judicial procedure. After a proposal to refer the bill to the Committee for the Insane, it was indefinitely postponed. This session also considered a bill which would prevent black people from testifying in a court of law. The *Oregon Statesman* summarized the discussion, without comment.

> . . . during the discussion in the House of the bill to amend the provisions of the code touching the qualification of witnesses, Mr. Fay desired section 701 to be amended so that the first clause should read as follows. "The following persons are not admissible: No person of African, Chinese, or Indian or [Hawaiian] blood, and persons of unsound mind, & etc." To this amendment Mr. Lawson of Yamhill County proposed to add the following: "It being the opinion of this Legislature that a Negro, Chinaman or Indian has no rights which a white man is bound to respect, and that a white man may murder, rob, rape, shoot, stab and cut any of those worthless, vagabond races,

> without being called to account thereof: Provided, he shall do said acts of bravery and chivalry when no white man is troubled by seeing the same."[10]

The bill was not passed.

In the closing years of the war, Oregon increased its support of the Union, and raised troops which were sent East. Oregon's role during the war was to protect the frontier from Indians and the interior from "rebel sympathizers," although the latter was not totally successful. In the election of November 1864, a sharp increase in population was noticed in the number of votes cast for the Democratic candidate for president. Most of the new arrivals were southern sympathizers from Missouri, dubbed the "left wing of Price's army," because many had deserted the Confederate army.[11] Many settled in southern and eastern Oregon and their numbers alarmed citizens, who feared that the balance of power in the legislature would shift back to the pro-slavery Democrats. Governor Addison C. Gibbs feared that at least 800 soldiers from the Confederate Army had settled in Oregon, and that others were on their way.

In July 1865, he received a petition from the citizens of Belpassi, Oregon, requesting that the legislature be called into a special session to ratify the Thirteenth Amendment. They wanted some protection from Southerners as well, saying:

> We would heartily encourage the emigration of good and loyal citizens to our adopted State, [but] feel assured it would be greatly detrimental to the peace and prosperity of Oregon to be overrun by hoards of disfranchised rebels and traitors.[12]

Gibbs called a special session, and addressed the opening meeting in a lengthy speech repeating the evils of slavery and endorsing the ratification of the Thirteenth Amendment. It was ratified in both chambers, but not without opposition. Dissenting members, all Democrats, argued that the people of Oregon had not been consulted and that the amendment had not been passed legally in Congress because the southern states were not represented. They also argued that it was a modification of the federal constitution and invaded state's rights.

In this session another half-hearted attempt to enforce the exclusion clause was proposed. Some members suggested that "successionists, guerillas, and bushwackers" should also be excluded.[13] This bill and a similar one proposed in 1866 failed to pass.

While the Civil War years saw political changes in Oregon, it did not improve the climate for black people who lived here. The Union party supported the North but continued to pass racist legislation. Advocates of slavery refused to admit defeat and during the Civil War united in an underground movement to support the South and establish slavery in Oregon.

In the southern part of the state, a die-hard pro-slavery group prepared plans to carve out a separate pro-South republic. The idea of creating a separate state in that area had been proposed as early as 1854, when the *Oregon Statesman* reported that a convention would be held in Jacksonville to consider creating another territory out of southern Oregon. Every effort would be made to resist joining the Union with the rest of Oregon Territory. Later that year a proposal was made to include northern California in the new territory, but was withdrawn when Joseph Lane received word that Californians objected to reducing the size of their state. During the constitutional convention in 1857, an amendment was offered to permit the creation of a separate state in southern Oregon, but this was defeated.

In 1861, secessionist sentiment found expression in the organization of a secret society that worked to defeat the pro-Union administration, resist the military draft, and plan the creation of a separate territory to be called the Pacific Coast Republic. This organization was part of a national group calling itself Knights of the Golden Circle. An underground group, it had secret passwords and signs by which members could recognize one another. One member would stroke his mustache twice with the first two fingers of the right hand closed against the thumb. The response was a scratch behind the ear with the right hand. A conversation followed:

"Were you out last night?"

"I were."

"Did you see that lone star?"

"I did."

"Which way did it point?"

"To the Southwest."

"Right, brother."[14]

According to information obtained through infiltrators, in 1863 and 1864 there were roughly 2,500 members in at least ten groups in various Oregon communities: two in Portland, two in Salem, and one each in Scio, Albany, Jacksonville and Yamhill County. They bought weapons and practiced military drills in secret. William Gwin, one of the California organizers of the Knights, wanted to model the Pacific Coast Republic after an ancient Venetian republic. Universal voting rights would be discarded and labor provided by Chinese, Hawaiians, and Negroes who would be imported and made slaves.

Many prominent Democrats were rumored to be members of this organization, including Joseph Lane. In Washington, D.C., he openly supported the Confederacy, suggesting that the North surrender and make peace. He returned to Oregon in disgrace, accused of smuggling guns for the Knights. In Dallas, Oregon, he was hung in effigy. His reception in Corvallis was more cordial and in a speech he affirmed his loyalty to the Union. Before he arrived at his home near Roseburg, he was injured by an accidental discharge from his rifle. He did not recover completely from the wound and spent the last twenty years of his life a recluse, deserted by all his friends. His last companion was a black youth, Peter Waldo, who lived with him in a cabin on the banks of the Umpqua River.

The Knights became openly militant in 1864, and it was rumored that members were well armed, particularly in the Long Tom and Siuslaw River valleys. Local pro-Union militia companies were organized and received weapons from the state arsenal, which was heavily guarded. Other secret societies called the Union League and Loyal League were formed to oppose the Knights. These groups never had a large membership, and when they attempted to organize a separate political platform in Multnomah County, internal division resulted and the organizations dissolved.

When it became clear that the North was winning the war, the Knights of the Golden Circle began to vanish. Strong local militia and informers within the organization insured against any attempt to seize power. By 1866, the *Oregonian* exposed the organization and its members, some of whom were running for public office.

> Voters of Oregon, do you want a United States Senator of that kind . . . who belonged to the treasonable Democratic organization of the "Old Guard?"[15]

During the Civil War, the legislature passed the last anti-black state laws, with the exception of the ban on intermarriage passed in 1866. Between 1866 and 1872, the legislature was required to consider ratification of the Fourteenth and Fifteenth Amendments, which gave citizenship to black people and the right to vote to black men. It was clear, however, that these amendments were unpopular with most Oregonians.

As early as 1843, Robert Newell, who had married an Indian woman, stated his objections to allowing black men to vote.

> I think we have got high enough among the dark clouds; I do not believe we ought to go any higher. It is well enough to admit the English, the French, the Spanish and the half-breeds, but the Indian and the Negro is a little too dark for me. I think we had better stop at the half-breeds. I am in favor of limiting the vote to them, and going no farther into the dark clouds to admit the Negro.[16]

In 1865, the *Oregonian* commented:

> The man who—knowing of the African race in our country—favors the extension of the privileges of citizenship to them, is surely reckless of the consequences, and regardless of the future result. . . . The Negroes as a class possess no capacity of self-government, and the few who are intelligent enough to take part in public affairs are offset by the multitude who don't. . . . this nation of the white race should well ponder the question before it admits the African, the Mongolian and the Indian to all its privileges.[17]

The *Oregon Statesman,* in an editorial published the same year, predicted that giving the vote to blacks would have a revolutionary influence on society.

> We do not believe that any democratic or republican form of government can successfully govern two separate and distinct races of people in large numbers with equal political rights to both races.[18]

Not only those few qualified blacks, but the masses just released from slavery would be able to vote. Full suffrage would result in a "war of the races," the editorial concluded.

> If we make the African a citizen, we cannot deny the same right to the Indian or the Mongolian (the Chinese, Japanese and other Asians). Then how long would we have peace and prosperity when four races separate, distinct and antagonistic, should be at the polls and contend for the control of government?[19]

The 1866 legislature, still controlled by the Union party but with a strong minority of Democrats, considered and ratified the Fourteenth Amendment, although the vote was close. When the resolution came up for discussion in the House, eighteen members entered a formal objection, claiming that the Judiciary Committee had recommended ratification without consulting two members. Two seats in the House were contested, and finally filled by the Democratic contenders. The Democrats made two attempts to withdraw ratification, but even with the support of the two additional Democrats, these attempts failed.

This legislature also passed another law prohibiting intermarriage. It was directed not only against white/black marriages, but against anyone with "one-fourth or more Negro, Chinese or [Hawaiian] blood, or any person having more than one-half Indian blood."[20] It was passed with little debate; the combined vote was forty-seven in favor, eight opposed and three absent. The penalty for disobeying the law was a prison sentence of not less than three months, or up to one year. Any person authorized to conduct marriages who broke the law by marrying two people illegally was subject to the same penalty, with an additional $1,000 fine. This law was not repealed until 1951.

The legislature's reluctance to endorse the Fourteenth Amendment was the subject of debate in the local press as well. In 1867, the Eugene *Weekly Democratic Review* printed a vicious attack on black people.

> . . . gaping, bullet pated, thick lipped, wooly headed animal jawed crowd of niggers, the dregs of broken up plantations, idle and vicious blacks, released from wholesome restraints of task masters and overseers . . . Greasy, dirty, lousy, they drowsily look down upon the assembled wisdom of a dissevered Union. Sleepily listen to legislators who have given them their freedom and now propose to invest them with the highest privileges of American citizenship.[21]

Because of its rabid pro-South rhetoric, this paper had been suppressed during the Civil War.

The editor of the *Oregonian,* who was called a "Negro Suffrage Pimp," by his counterpart at the *Oregon Statesman,* accused the Democrats of trading on fears of intermarriage to force defeat of the Fifteenth Amendment.[22]

> For that class tell us and have told us for many years that the recognition of any rights to the Negro race would infallibly lead to enforced social equality and to compel white people to marry "niggers."[23]

In 1868, another attempt was made to repeal ratification of the Fourteenth Amendment, declared to be ratified nationally only six weeks previously. This time the repeal passed in both chambers by a combined vote of thirty-nine to twenty-seven. This session also recalled Oregon Senators George H. Williams and Henry W. Corbett, criticized for their support of Reconstruction. Williams was also active in a campaign to impeach President Andrew Johnson, who had become the hero of the Democratic party for his opposition to Reconstruction. The legislature was not deluded into thinking that its actions would make any difference; the *Oregonian* predicted that if copies of the resolutions ever reached Congress they would probably be used to light someone's cigar. The actions of the legislature prompted the *Oregonian* to remind its readers of the Democrats' notorious sympathy for the South, and the following headlines were printed:

> SPECIAL DISPATCH TO THE OREGONIAN: THE ACT CONSUMMATED—PASSAGE OF THE SECESSION ORDINANCE BY THE OREGON SENATE! THE DEMOCRATIC PARTY REPUDIATE THE CONSTITUTION—OREGON OUT OF THE UNION![24]

The Fifteenth Amendment was proposed, ratified and declared in force by Congress between Oregon's 1868 and 1870 legislative sessions. No special session was called to ratify the amendment, and Governor Lafayette Grover said in his inaugural address,

> I shall not forbear placing on record my settled conviction that the two propositions last promulgated as amendments to the Constitution of the U.S.—effecting, as they do, such violence to the inherent and reserved rights of the several States—have never been legally sanctioned. And while we yield to superior force, exercised by the will of her people, let our Constitution stand, sustained by the will of her people, as a living landmark to the former dignity of the States of the Union, and as a land-mark to American liberty.[25]

The legislative session of 1870 affirmed the governor's sentiments, declaring that the Fifteenth Amendment was "an infringement on popular rights and a direct falsification of the pledges made to the state of Oregon by the federal government."[26] Grover's "landmark to American liberty" remained for eighty-nine years, until the Fifteenth Amendment was finally ratified by the centennial legislature of 1959.

Although Oregon refused to ratify the Fifteenth Amendment, a state Supreme Court decision rendered in 1870 affirmed the right of black men to vote. The case involved the election of a county commissioner in Wasco County, and C. H. Yates and W. S. Ford, two black men who had voted. The court confirmed the legality of their votes, saying,

> We cannot do otherwise than declare it to be a valid amendment to the federal Constitution. To hold otherwise would be to unwarrantably overthrow certain well established principles of law, and give to judicial

> discussion such a coloring of partisan feeling as would lead to very unfortunate results.[27]

In April 1870, the *Oregon Herald*, a short-lived Portland newspaper, reported that three black men were allowed to vote at a local school meeting, and then commented:

> Can the judges of the election, at the school meeting the other night, show any authority for receiving the votes of negroes? The judges who received said vote . . . exhibited indecent haste in forcing an odious measure down the throats of the people of Oregon.[28]

The same year the *Oregonian*, which five years earlier had contained editorials opposing the Fifteenth Amendment, ran an editorial which admitted:

> There are but a few colored men in Oregon, and their political influence cannot be great. But these here are, as a rule, quiet, industrious and intelligent citizens. We cannot doubt they will exercise intelligently the franchise with which they are newly invested.[29]

The black population of Oregon was small and nearly invisible. With the exception of the ban on intermarriage passed in 1866, the legislature did not pass laws that discriminated against local black people. Resistance to civil rights legislation both national and local was strong; in the five years following the Civil War any measure that promoted civil rights for black people elicited the charge that it would promote racial intermarriage. In order to kill any legislation, opponents had only to ask the perennial question: "Do you want your daughter to marry a nigger?"[30]

In spite of legislation that guaranteed access to public schools for all children, segregation was briefly practiced in the 1860s and 1870s in Portland, Salem, and Pendleton. In 1867 William Brown, a black resident of Portland, attempted to enroll his four children in public school. The director of the school refused to admit the children, and Brown applied to a white man, T. A. Wood, for help. Wood approached the director and was informed that if the black children were admitted the school would lose its funding. The director proposed that the amount of money allocated for each child, amounting to $2.25 per quarter, be set aside to rent a building and hire a teacher to instruct the black children. Wood objected, reasoning that only $35.00 dollars could be raised this way and that the black parents would have to make up the difference out of their own pockets. He filed an appeal in court, which was decided in favor of the school. The school board agreed to allocate $800 for a separate school and in the fall of 1867 a school for black children was opened.

The next year $1,000 was allocated for the black school and for the next three years twenty-five black children were enrolled. In 1870 several black children requested admittance to the regular public school but were sent home. At the annual school board meeting in 1871 it was agreed to continue the separate school, but one year later it was discontinued. In 1874 thirty black children were enrolled in the public schools.

In 1873 J. B. Mitchell, a black barber who lived in Pendleton, sent his two children to public school. The children were refused admittance and the teacher, a strong segregationist, closed the school. White families paid for a private school which was set up over the county jail. A rival barbershop was opened in an attempt to drive the black family out of town, but they persisted and eventually the children were taught in public school.

The black residents of Salem organized an evening school in 1868 and placed an announcement in the local newspaper.

> Notice is hereby given that the colored people of Salem expect to pay all the expenses of the Evening School now being held by them, without aid from other citizens—No person is authorized to collect funds in our name.[31]

Salem also had a separate grammar school for black children in 1871. The school was located on the corner of High and Marion and built at a cost of $1,200, but by 1874 it was not in use and the black children were attending public school.

In 1860, in spite of the fact that Oregon had entered the Union with a free state constitution, Oregonians were still electing known pro-slavery leaders to high political office. This love affair with the right wing Democratic party ended only when it became clear that the alternative they proposed, secession from the Union, was untenable. The war forced Oregonians to choose sides, and they did so, reluctantly. The Union party gained a majority in the state legislature, but continued to pass racist legislation. Uncomfortable with the radical solutions embodied in the Civil War amendments to the federal Constitution, their opposition was demonstrated in resolutions that had little more than sentimental value. Resistance to accepting the black vote and integrated education was overcome not by a change in attitude, but because Oregonians realized that federal civil rights legislation had to be acknowledged, if not endorsed.

By 1870, change was inevitable, so Oregonians acquiesced. Blacks were granted civil rights under the terms imposed by the federal government, without the endorsement of the state legislature. Oregon's black population was small and posed little threat to the established order. The period of enacting racist legislation had ended, but it would be many years before the legislature would begin to take an interest in passing laws that would allow black people to enjoy equal rights as citizens of the state.

6

A Few Colored Men in Oregon

Blacks in Oregon 1850–1900

Despite persistent racist attitudes that existed in Oregon, expressed in exclusion laws, attitudes toward slavery and a strong reluctance to accept federal legislation after the Civil War, a few black people settled in the state. Many had come with white families and chose to remain. Some lived in the rural areas of Oregon, but by the turn of the century 70 percent were living in Portland.

Black people who lived in the rural areas of Oregon in the nineteenth century faced special problems of isolation and vulnerability, but sometimes enjoyed a greater degree of social acceptance among their white neighbors than did their urban contemporaries. Evidence exists documenting open racism in small towns in that century, and it has not disappeared. In 1893 the citizens of Liberty, Oregon, requested that all the black people leave town. News of this prompted the suggestion that the town change its name.[1] More than eighty years later a news item reported that residents of Curry County vetoed federal money for low cost housing because "all the niggers will move down from Portland."[2] Isolated black people occasionally left a mark on the area in which they lived in local place names, although these too are evidence of racist attitudes. These include "Darky Creek," "Nigger Brown Canyon," "Nigger Rock," and "Nigger Creek Bar."[3]

The treatment that rural black people received varied from place to place and depended in part on the size of the black population and the attitudes of their white neighbors. In Jacksonville, where residents were hostile toward minorities, blacks and Chinese were treated in an outrageous manner. In Canyon City, where the black population was much smaller, racial discrimination was not widely practiced, and one black family that lived there was treated with a measure of respect.

The isolation of the rural black family was sometimes an advantage, and in the few family histories that have been preserved a pattern of respect and a measure of social equality emerges. Isolated black families often prospered where their numbers posed no threat to the white community. Some of these families or individuals were able to live more independently than blacks in the urban community: they owned land, worked for themselves, and prospered. Accounts of their lives frequently mention the positive contributions they made in the community, aiding families in times of trouble and nursing the sick, especially in isolated areas where doctors were unavailable.

Much of the documentation of their lives is missing, or has died with the memory of those who knew them. What is left is largely an oral tradition, supplemented or contradicted by scattered evidence in census reports, birth, death, marriage and land sale records. It is in this context that the history of their lives will be told.

Robin and Polly Holmes came to Oregon with Nathaniel Ford in 1844. The conditions under which they came, whether slave or free, were disputed in the court case over the custody of their children, and continues to be disputed by Ford's descendants, who insist that Robin and Polly begged Ford to allow them to come to Oregon with him.[4]

The two families lived together for a time, and Robin raised vegetables to sell to his neighbors. Around 1850 they moved to Nesmith Mills, where Robin obtained work. In 1854 his name appeared on a Polk County tax record which listed the total value of his personal property at $655. Later they moved to Salem, and established a small nursery, selling fruit trees and shrubs. Ford and a Dr. Boyle bought a lot and constructed a home for the family; after Robin died Polly continued to live there with her son, Lon. In 1864 he was accused of a theft and nearly hanged. He died soon after.

In spite of the court case, Ford's descendants insist that relationships between the two families remained cordial. Roxanna Holmes once visited a granddaughter of Nathaniel Ford in Portland, to say how thankful she was for all the help the Ford family had given them.[5]

Mary Jane Holmes, their eldest daughter, was born in Missouri in 1841, and came to Oregon as a young child. Although the court awarded custody of the children to their parents, when Mary Jane married Reuben Shipley in 1857, Ford demanded that a sum of money be paid in exchange for her freedom.[6] In spite of advice given to Reuben by his white friends, Eldridge Hartless, the Reverend T.J. Conner, and others, Reuben agreed to pay Ford a sum of money in order to marry the woman he loved.[a] J.B. Hinkle, a friend

a It should be mentioned that Reuben Shipley (born 1811) was forty-six years old when he married the sixteen-year-old Mary Jane Holmes (born 1841).

and business associate of Robert Shipley, the son of Reuben's old master, said that $700 was given to Ford.[7]

Reuben Shipley had been born a slave in Kentucky around 1800. He took the surname of his master, Robert Shipley, a common practice. His skills were highly respected, and he became overseer of a large plantation in Missouri, and was entrusted with the education of his master's son, Robert Shipley, Jr. While in Missouri he married a woman from a nearby plantation and had two sons. He came to Oregon with the Shipley family in the 1850s, deciding to leave his wife and children in exchange for a promise of freedom. After completing his contract with his master he was given his freedom. In the meantime, his wife had died, and the man who owned his two sons refused to allow Reuben to buy their freedom. Eldridge Hartless gave him a job, and Reuben saved $1500 to buy eighty acres of land between Corvallis and Philomath. On this farm he settled with his new wife, Mary Jane. They raised a family of three girls and three boys.

The family was well liked and entered into the social life of the community, attending a nearby church. When another settler, William Wyatt, suggested that a high part of the Shipley farm would be a good spot for a cemetery, Reuben agreed to deed two acres to the county, on the condition that black people could be buried there. In 1861 the transaction was completed and the original land of Mt. Union Cemetery was transferred to Benton County. Twelve years later, Reuben and one daughter, who had died of smallpox while visiting relatives in Salem, were buried there.

In 1875 Mary Jane married R.G. Drake. They lived in Corvallis until his death a few years later. In 1880 Mary Jane was living in east Salem with her younger children, Nettie and Charles. She may have returned to her Corvallis farm, for neighbors recalled her helpfulness during the typhoid epidemics in the 1880s. In 1889 she sold the farm and moved to Portland, where her remaining son, Edward, was employed by the Southern Pacific Railroad. She spent her remaining years there until her death in 1925, when she was taken back to Corvallis to be buried next to her two husbands and children in Mt. Union Cemetery.

William (John) Livingston was born in 1836, and came to Oregon in 1864 with the Judge Ringo family as a free man. He was born the son of slaves in Missouri, and at about the age of twelve was sold to a family who lived in Hannibal, Missouri. There he became the playmate, so it is claimed, of Samuel Clemens, a boy one year his senior, who was later to write under the pen name of Mark Twain.[8] He later was sold to Joseph Ringo for $850, and remained with him after he was freed in 1863.

During the Civil War, rumors were widespread that Union soldiers were forcing slaves to leave their masters. The Ringo family, an older black woman called "Aunt Lucy," a young boy named Andy, and William Livingston, or John as he was always known, came to Oregon. They went first to Nebraska, with John concealed in a big wooden box for fear the Union soldiers would discover him.

According to the family history, Judge Ringo gave John forty acres of land between Oregon City and Molalla, in an area known as Clarkes. In 1876 he married Alice Cooper, a young black woman about seventeen years old. She too had been born in Missouri, and had come to Oregon in 1861 with a family who settled near Albany. They had one son, Charles.

In 1891, Alice Cooper Livingston died and was buried in the Clarkes cemetery, on land originally owned by Judge Ringo. According to family tradition, the first person to be buried in this cemetery was Ringo's cook, the black woman named Aunt Lucy.

John Livingston lived until 1912. At the time of his death, he owned the forty acres given him by Ringo and an additional 180 acres in eastern Oregon. His estate was valued at $15,000. He was well known in Clackamas County, and remained close friends with the Ringo family, always bringing the children candy in old-fashioned striped bags.

A Justice of the Peace in Clackamas County named Mr. Samson, a close friend who handled John's correspondence because he could not read or write said of him,

> I never knew a finer man than John Livingston. He was the soul of honor. His skin was as black as coal but his heart was alabaster. His word was gospel, and I have often heard the bankers of the city say they would rather have John Livingston's word than that of any white man in the county in a financial transaction.[9]

He was buried beside his wife, beneath an ornate marble stone in the Clarkes cemetery. Hundreds of people attended his funeral.

Lou Southworth was born in Tennessee around 1830. His father's name was Hunter, but he was born into slavery and took the surname of his master, James Southworth. His early life was spent in Franklin County, Missouri and he emigrated to Oregon with his mother and James Southworth in the 1850s. He lived on an abandoned claim for a time, with his master living with him because times were so hard. While mining gold in Jacksonville, he sent money to his master toward the purchase of his freedom. He fought in the Rogue River Indian wars without compensation. Meeting a company of volunteer soldiers on their way to the Rogue River, he was asked to give up his rifle, as weapons were scarce. Not wishing to lose the gun, he joined the company. His mother died at the age of seventy, and Lou moved to Yreka, California, where he made a living playing the violin for dancing schools. The money he made playing the violin completed payment, $1,000 in all, for his freedom.

In 1868 he moved to Buena Vista, Oregon, and worked as a blacksmith. There he learned to read and write, and joined the Victoria Lodge of Masons. He married and in 1880 moved with his wife and stepson to Tidewater, near Waldport, where his wife died six years later. He lived and worked on the Alsea River, ferrying passengers and cargo up and down the river. In the summers he worked near Philomath and Corvallis, helping with the hay harvest to earn money for winter supplies.

He was known as a man who always voted. In 1880, on election day, a storm was blowing across Alsea Bay, and everyone was afraid to cross the bay to vote. Lou rigged up oil cans on the front and back of his boat to provide extra flotation, and braved the storm. He was the only one to cross the bay that day. A religious man, he loved to play the violin, as it comforted him during lonely hours. The local church objected to his playing, so he stopped attending church. He died in Corvallis in 1917.

His stepson, Alvin McCleary, spent most of his life near the Alsea River. Born in San Francisco in 1866, his mother had died when he was a baby and he was adopted by the woman who later became Lou Southworth's wife.[b] In 1896, he began fishing commercially, and also worked as a butcher in Newport. He was well respected in the community:

> A Negro gentleman named Alvin McCleary was a respected businessman and city councilman in Waldport, where I was raised. As a school boy I never heard one harsh word said against Alvin even in the rugged days of the K.K.K.[10]

Alvin McCleary died in Corvallis in his eighties.

Among the settlers who came to Oregon in 1843 was Daniel Waldo, who emigrated in the same party as Jesse Applegate. Like Peter Burnett, who came to Oregon the same year, Waldo served on the Legislative Committee of 1844 and voted in favor of the exclusion law passed in the June session. Despite this vote, Waldo had come to Oregon with his family and a number of black people, including a daughter, America Waldo, whose mother was

b Her name was Mary Cooper.

a slave.[c] He settled in the hills east of Salem building a house with separate quarters for his slaves.

In January 1863, America married Richard A. Bogle, and moved to Walla Walla. Richard A. Bogle was born in the West Indies in 1835, emigrating to New York at the age of twelve. He crossed the plains to Oregon with James Cogswell, arriving in 1851. After a three year stay he moved to Yreka, California, and apprenticed himself to a barber, Nathaniel Ferber, for the next three years. After a mining stint near Deadwood California, he returned to Oregon and maintained a barber shop in Roseburg. In 1862 he moved to Walla Walla, Washington. He mined in Florence, Elk City and Orofino, then bought a barber shop in Walla Walla and continued his trade. He was a wealthy man with ranching interests, and was one of the founders of the Walla Walla Savings and Loan Association. America and Richard Bogle had eight children, including a son, Arthur, who had a barber shop in Portland in the early 1900s. Descendants of the family include Richard Waldo Bogle, Sr., and his son, Richard Waldo Bogle, Jr. of Portland.[11]

Daniel Delaney, Sr. came to Oregon in 1843 with his family and a black woman, Rachel Beldon. He settled near the farm of Daniel Waldo east of Salem in an area that has come to be called the Waldo Hills. Delaney had lived in east Tennessee where he owned a plantation and a number of slaves. He sold his slaves and land, purchased Rachel for $1,000 and brought her to Oregon, where she worked in the fields, maintained the household and garden, and nursed Mrs. Delaney, who was an invalid for many years.

Despite the fact that Oregon had banned slavery, Rachel continued to live with Delaney until the close of the Civil War, when her freedom was assured. She had two sons, Newman and Jack, and later married a black man, Nathan Brooks. They lived on the farm of Daniel Waldo before moving to Salem.

Daniel Delaney, Sr., was murdered on his farm in 1865, by two men who blackened their faces and posed as Negroes, as Delaney was known to be friendly to black people. He had recently sold a large number of cattle, and robbery appeared to be the motive for his killing. The only witness was a black boy, Jack De Wolf, who was Delaney's servant and companion. Jack managed to escape undetected, hid in a woodpile all night, and the next

c Daniel Waldo arrived alone in Oregon in 1843 to establish his land claim. America, born in 1844, and her mother were enslaved by one of Daniel's brothers, Joseph or John. The identity of her father is unknown, but Bogle family sources claim it was one of the Waldo brothers. In 1854, America, and perhaps other enslaved Blacks, came to Oregon with John Waldo's widow Avarilla. It appears America lived as a free member of the Waldo family in Oregon. Her wedding to Richard Bogle in Salem was controversial for taking place in a white church before a mixed-race congregation, and for having a white officiant, the Congregationalist minister Obed Dickinson. See Brian W. Williams, "America Waldo Bogle: Her Early Life and the Question of her Ancestry" and Nokes (2013).

day ran to the neighboring farm of Daniel Delaney, Jr. to report what had happened.[d]

Jack's testimony helped to convict the murderers, who were hanged in Salem a few months later. No one in Salem would claim their bodies, so Daniel Waldo agreed to bury the men on his farm. For many years a fence surrounded the graves of the first men to die for committing a crime in Marion County.[12]

Gold was discovered in Jacksonville in the early 1850s, and a bustling town soon sprang up. Among the settlers who came to the area were a number of black people. The census of 1860 lists forty-two blacks living in Jackson County. Conditions were rough, and most did not stay long. Racial incidents were common, and black people were jailed on any excuse.

The journals of Thomas Fletcher Royal, the first county school superintendent, record two examples of the treatment black people received. In 1853, he reported that while he was away on business a black girl tried to attend public school. White parents refused to allow their children to attend school, as one person related to Royal:

> Their parents can not bear the thought of sending their children to school with a Negro—it will be throwed up to them as long as they live.[13]

The girl had to stop attending school, as it was more than the town could stand.

In 1854, the local church was in danger of being mobbed because a black man was allowed to preach and pray with the congregation. Royal's diary preserves one such incident:

> We could often smell the cigars and whisky about the window and hear the rowdies run and yell out curses as they stood around listening or as they fled mocking. Again they would be ready to mob us for allowing a colored brother, Isaac Jones, a local preacher, to come into our meetings and pray with us. They swore they would take Isaac out if we called on him again, and cursed us for being abolitionists. But we hardly ever failed to call on brother Jones at every prayer meeting. For he was full of faith and the Holy Ghost, and when he prayed we always felt manifestations of divine power.[14]

---

d After marrying and obtaining her freedom, Rachel Belden Brooks sued the Delaney estate for $10,000 for uncompensated services of her and her son Noah to Daniel Delaney. She was awarded $1,000. See Craig Smith and Delaney Yoder Smith, "Rachel Belden Delaney Brooks," Willamette Valley Genealogical Society "Beaver Briefs" 51, no. 2 (2019).

Another black man, Mat Banks, was brought before the local court on a charge of disturbing the peace. His neighbors complained that he was praying and singing hymns too loudly. The court freed him, but several months later he was brought before the court again on the same charge. This time the court decided that he was insane, and he was committed to the state asylum.[15]

After the gold mines were exhausted, most black people went elsewhere. Those who remained became farmers or worked as blacksmiths, carpenters, barbers, washerwomen, shinglemakers, etc. Three men about whom some information has been preserved were perhaps typical.

Samuel Cozzens was born in Virginia in 1822, and came to Jackson County in the 1870s. He was a woodcutter, bought and sold land, and died in 1891. Jackson Berry was born in Tennessee in 1818, and came to Oregon in 1852. He apparently came with a white man named H.A. Overbeck, who agreed to free him after ten years of service in Oregon. In 1866 he filed a land claim for 112 acres, and in 1872 received title to the land. He remained in Jackson County, working as a farmer, until his death in 1892. Samuel Vose was born in Massachusetts in 1812 and came to Jacksonville in the 1850s or 1860s. In 1861 he sold his house and land. For many years he was a barber and bootblack in the Elite Barbershop on Main Street in Jacksonville. In 1879 he traded his house and land to Jeanne Holt in exchange for room and board in the hotel she built on his land. He lived there rent free until his death in 1882. The barberpole from his shop is still on display in the Jacksonville museum. Cozzens, Berry and Vose were buried in a separate section of the Jacksonville cemetery reserved for black people.

Gold was discovered in 1862 on Canyon Creek by men searching for the fabled "Blue Bucket Mine," and a town soon grew up. Eight million dollars was taken from Canyon City mines in the 1870s and the town had a population of 10,000. Among those who came to the boom town called Canyon City was a black man, Columbus Sewell, and his wife. Born in 1820 in Virginia, he had served in the Black Hawk War under General Scott. He came to California during the gold rush, and moved to Canyon City in the 1860s. After operating a mining claim for a time, he turned to hauling freight for his livelihood. His wife, Louisa, was born in Richmond, Virginia. They had three sons, two of whom survived into adulthood. Louisa was remembered for the delicious ice cream she made, and was fond of entertaining her neighbors. She built a park and croquet court opposite their home, and entertained visitors on the 4th of July with ice cream and cake. She died in 1893, visited during her last illness by many of the ladies of the town.

The couple's eldest son, Thomas, entered the freighting business, and lived in Canyon City until his death in the 1940s. He married Cora Misette in 1899. They had no children, and Cora died in 1919. Later, he married a Portland woman, but continued to live in Canyon City. During the 1930s he was sentenced to a term in the State Penitentiary for selling whiskey to an Indian, but according to those who knew him he expressed no ill feelings, and regarded the experience as an adventure. He got to ride a train, was given a new set of dentures, and regular meals and clothing. He was well liked and respected, and frequently aided his neighbors in times of illness, in some cases acting as nurse. He died during a visit to Portland, and was brought back to be buried in the Canyon City cemetery.

Joseph Sewell, his younger brother, was an attractive rogue and an excellent horseman and athlete, addicted to the wild and wooly aspects of frontier life, where drinking, racing and fighting were daily events. As a child, he was for a time the best fighter in the area, and took on all challengers. His exploits made entertaining reading in the local paper:

> A true specimen of the Sunny South gave Tiger town a call last Friday. After getting the usual amount of tangle-foot he started to take the town, and after the leading sporting man of John Day had tried to knock him out of time according to the latest revised rules of Tiger town, and failed, our colored friend was introduced to Justice Kelly, who taxed him $12.50 for the benefit of the public school. He was sent on his way rejoicing.
>
> Spring fights have already begun. Joe Sewell last Monday slapped a fellow called 'Frenchy' for using insulting language towards his mother. Joe was arrested, but the case was compromised by each paying half the costs.[16]

Joseph Sewell died in the 1890s, according to some as a result of a fight in Baker, according to others in a brawl in a Pendleton whorehouse.

One of the earliest black residents of Portland was Abner Hunt Francis, who with his wife, Lynda[e], settled in Portland in the early 1850s. Under the 1849 exclusion law, still in effect, he was living in Portland illegally, but over 200 people signed a petition urging that he be allowed to remain. Although the law was not repealed until 1854, the couple remained in Portland. In 1852 they ran a boarding house, and Ezra Meeker, an early resident, remarked on their hospitality.

---

e Her name was Sydna Edmonia Robella Francis (née Dandridge).

In the mid-1850s Francis owned a mercantile store on the corner of Front and Stark, advertising the lowest rates offered in Portland on such goods as wool plaid, French merino, silk dress goods, fashionable bonnets and mantillas and an assortment of furs, as well as groceries, cement and glass. His store also advertised sheet music furnished on two weeks' notice at San Francisco prices. The *Weekly Oregonian* carried a large notice for weeks advertising the business, which made Francis a wealthy man. By 1860 his real and personal property was valued at $36,000.

In late 1860 the couple left Portland on the *Brother Jonathan* and arrived in Victoria B.C. on October 9. The sale of his Portland business resulted in a loss, and Francis was forced to declare bankruptcy in 1862. His reasons for leaving Portland are unknown, but Victoria contained a thriving black population, supplemented by ex-California blacks who left the United States because of racism.[f] A. H. Francis was introduced to the U. S. Speaker of the House, Schuyler Colfax, who visited Victoria in 1865. He remained in Victoria until his death in 1872.[17]

By 1870, 47 percent of the black population of Oregon lived in Multnomah County.[18] Twenty years later, the population of Portland, including the unincorporated cities of East Portland and Albina, included 519 black people, 44 percent of the total black population of the state. They composed less than 1 percent of the total population of Portland, which at that time was 62,046. Most lived on the west side of the river, scattered within an area from S. W. Montgomery to N. W. Kearney, and from the river west to 12th Street. A few lived in Albina and East Portland.[19]

Most of the racist sentiment in Portland during this period was directed against the Chinese, the largest minority in the city. In 1880 Portland had the second largest Chinese population in the nation, and in 1890 there were a total of 4,740 Chinese and 20 Japanese living in the Portland area.[20] Most lived on the west side of the river. By contrast, the black population of Portland in 1890 was only 519, with 92 percent living on the west side. Racial antagonism toward the Chinese population was common, as a modern Portland historian observed:

> The year of 1886 was rough for Portland's Chinese, especially in March, 1886. Raids, beatings, arson fires were common. Labor was

f Abner Hunt Francis was an abolitionist. He wrote letters from Portland to his friend Frederick Douglass, detailing the racism he witnessed in Oregon and California. Blacks in California began a mass immigration to Victoria, BC, in 1858; among the immigrants were Sydna's parents, John and Charlotte Dandridge. After a visit to Victoria in 1860, the couple determined their family had better prospects in Canada than the United States. They arrived in Victoria aboard the steamer *Sierra Nevada*—not the more famous *Brother Jonathan*—in August 1861. See Kenneth Hawkins, "'A Proper Attitude of Resistance': The Oregon Letters of A. H. Francis to Frederick Douglass, 1851–1860," *Oregon Historical Quarterly* 121, no. 4 (Winter 2020).

> the main culprit. Public animosity was inflamed by politicians such as Sylvester Pennoyer who ran for Governor, and won on an anti-Chinese plank. Oregon's U. S. Senator John H. Mitchell gave demagogic speeches on the Senate floor.[21]

Out of a total of 285 black people listed in Portland's city directories for the years between 1864 and 1887, the highest number of people were employed in jobs relating to the restaurant, saloon and hotel industry. A few owned businesses, but the majority were stewards, waiters, cooks and porters. The next largest number of people were employed in the shoe and bootmaker trades and clothing manufacturing, with many also employed as bootblacks and dressmakers. 16.3 percent were employed as laborers or jobbers. 13 percent were barbers or hairdressers. The rest held jobs as domestics, janitors, house cleaners, laundresses, whitewashers, messengers, expressmen, packers, steamboatmen, apprentices, and gardeners. A handful listed their occupations as student, physician, nurse, pastor and music teacher. The two most common jobs were cooks and bootblacks.

In 1883 a group of black people marched in a parade in Portland to celebrate the completion of a rail line from the East Coast to Portland. It was a significant event for black people, as the railroad offered new employment opportunities. Soon black porters, dining car waiters and other railroad employees came to settle in Portland.

The Portland Hotel had been started and then abandoned in the 1880s. When it was completed in 1890, over one million dollars, most of it put up by Portland's wealthy class, had been spent to complete the eight floor, 326 room hotel. For three decades it was the center of the business and social life of the city. Approximately seventy-five black men were brought from North and South Carolina and Georgia to work in the hotel as barbers, waiters, and in other positions. The wages and tips paid these men allowed them to send for their families. They formed the elite of Portland's black community, and some were able to leave the hotel to go into business for themselves. Many families were also able to purchase homes.

Those black people that went into business for themselves often succeeded by serving the needs of the black community. Some operated boarding houses, restaurants, saloons, barbershops and hotels.

One of the most lucrative opportunities for blacks as well as whites was in the underworld that flourished in Portland in the late nineteenth century, tolerated by a corrupt city government. Gambling and prostitution were practiced openly; the police force took bribes and ignored illegal activities. The "redlight" district was originally located on the west side, between

Burnside, Broadway, Glisan and the Willamette River. In this section there was more racial intermingling; Japanese, French, white and black women were employed as prostitutes in houses, or worked as waitresses and dancers. Black men owned saloons and gambling houses. Many prominent white citizens had a financial interest in the area, and blacks made money and were able to wield political influence. Bribery was an accepted practice, and black businessmen were often paid to deliver the black vote. Occasionally, when the parties were divided, it became possible for the black politicians to collect from both sides. During this time a black barber named Charlie Green was put up for city councilman and elected by the Democrats. He never took his seat, as he was bought off.[22]

After the Emancipation Proclamation, Oregon's black citizens organized annual celebrations to mark their freedom, as did black people around the country. In January of 1868, one celebration was held in Salem, attended by local black people, as well as residents of Albany and the surrounding area, and white people from both political parties. The local paper reported that among the numbers attending were six blacks who had been freed by the Proclamation; A. Boles, a blacksmith, presided and the event was celebrated with prayers, singing, reciting poems, and concluded with a social dance and supper.[23]

A similar celebration was held the following year in Portland. Although neither the *Oregonian* or the *Oregon Herald* sent reporters to cover the event, they both published accounts of it. The *Oregon Herald* reported,

> We were not present, but we are told that the exercises were highly creditable to the darkies . . .[24]

In 1870, black people had something additional to celebrate: the ratification of the Fifteenth Amendment. During this celebration a "declaration of sentiments" was prepared and read in which Abraham Lincoln was eulogized, black people pleaded their loyalty and resolved:

> That it shall be our chief aim to render such an account of ourselves, should our country need us, that America the greatest nation of the earth, may be proud of her newly enfranchised citizens.[25]

In 1870 there were other brief news items about the black community. Black citizens that year voiced a protest that their children were excluded from the annual Sunday School picnic. Ben Holiday, a flashy and unscrupulous railroad man who financed Republican elections, attempted to buy the black vote and his maneuvers were reported in detail. But interest in the black vote and the new status of the black citizen soon died, and the press turned its attention elsewhere.

The first black church in Portland was organized in 1862 and met for a time at the home of Mrs. Mary Carr, who owned a boarding house on First Street. It was then called the People's Church, and services were held in the homes of various members. In January 1869, the African Methodist Episcopal Zion Church was incorporated in Portland, and property was purchased on N.W. Third Street, between Burnside and Couch. The first pastor of the church was the Reverend J. O. Lodge. In 1883 the congregation erected a building on Thirteenth and Main, and remained there until 1916, when the congregation moved to the east side of the river and built a church on Williams Avenue.

In 1895 the California African Methodist Episcopal Conference sent the Reverend S.S. Freeman to Portland to establish an A.M.E. Church. Meetings were first held in a building donated by a Mr. Jenkin, a black man who owned a building on Thirteenth and Everett. This arrangement ended when the pastor offended Mr. Jenkin by marrying his daughter to a porter on the Southern Pacific Railroad. The newlyweds left town, and Mr. Freeman was forced to find another place to conduct church services.

He and his wife opened a boarding house for railroad people between Third and Fourth on Everett Street. This venture was successful, and soon the congregation, called the Bethel A.M.E. Church, was able to buy the Japanese mission building on Tenth Street between Everett and Davis. The church remained at this location until 1916, when it moved to the east side and built a church on Larrabee and McMillen.

A third black church, the Mount Oliver Baptist Church, was established in Portland in the 1890s. When it moved to the east side and built a church on First and Schuyler, the lumber used to construct the building was donated by a local branch of the Ku Klux Klan.[26]

Some of Portland's blacks believed that they were more fortunate than their southern counterparts, and in 1879 organized a society to encourage black people to move to Oregon. Called the Portland Colored Immigration Society, the organization printed a circular which was distributed to southern and southwestern states, giving information on the climate, products and resources of Oregon. The society proposed to raise funds to purchase tickets for black people wishing to come to Oregon, and to provide temporary housing and give advice and other information to black people newly arrived.

Political clubs and fraternal organizations were also established, growing out of an awareness of the need to unite and enhance what little political power black people had. Discouragement, the pressures of earning a living, and internal divisions often meant that these associations did not last long.

By the turn of the century, black people in Oregon were beginning to initiate efforts to improve their political and social condition. The New Port Republican Club wielded enough influence to secure the placement of a black man, George Hardin, on the police force in 1894. Black people were beginning to go to the state legislature to lobby for the repeal of the exclusion clause and the ban on voting, and to secure the repeal of the law prohibiting interracial marriages.[27]

7

Sober, Industrious and Honest

The Black Community in Portland

January 1, 1900, marked the beginning of a new century, and optimism reigned. Black people in Portland could assess their accomplishments with pride. The small, struggling community had seen some progress and the beginnings of change. Churches and other social institutions were established, and the effort to secure the repeal of racist laws had at least begun. Two years later, they were reminded of the task that lay ahead of them:

> It has been difficult for the colored race to get a right start, and [it] is also difficult for many of them yet to realize the necessity of right living and earnest steady efforts for their betterment, and to prepare themselves for the duties and responsibilities of citizenship.[1]

Between 1890 and 1900 the number of black people in Oregon had decreased slightly, from 1,186 to 1,105, but in the same decade the proportion of the black population living in Multnomah County rose from 44 percent to 70 percent, drawn by increased job opportunities at the Portland Hotel and with the railroads. Since 1896, they had a voice in the press in the person of A.D. Griffin, owner and publisher of the *New Age*. Griffin had been the editor of the Spokane *Northwest Echo* before corning to Portland, and was a prominent Mason. While living in Oregon, he became the first black man to attend a Republican state convention, and was a stockholder in the Enterprise Investment Company.

Published weekly, the *New Age* was not designed to appeal strictly to a black audience; the front page carried general news from the national telegraphic services. News of specific interest to black people was featured on the inside pages and the editorial page. The paper reflected the activities of the local black community and also contained news of black people throughout the Northwest and in the rest of the nation. Coverage was given to events in the South; lynchings and other racist activities were reported as well as news about the accomplishments of black people. Advertisements were often solicited from white-owned businesses, which Griffin urged his readers to patronize. Black-owned businesses advertised in the paper as well.

The newspaper reflected the political and social point of view of its editor. He was an image-maker, and wanted the black people of Oregon to be "sober, industrious and honest," believing that when all members of the race lived up to this standard a measure of economic, if not social equality would be forthcoming.[2] The paper contained advice, examples, praise and criticism of black people based on this standard of behavior. When the federal census was taken in 1900 Griffin urged black people to report home ownership, even if they had made only one payment. He reprinted statements from Booker T. Washington advising black people to declare the value of all their personal property to the census enumerators so that the number and wealth of the national black population could be determined. After the census results were published, Griffin had this advice:

> The Negro should remember that he has rights, but also that, after all, he as a whole is not equal in all respects to the whites, and therefore he has duties to himself and his successors to perform a duty to the race . . . Let the colored man remember that he is one of nine millions . . . with a consciousness, an eye, an ear, a tongue, and a hand that are not to be despised and must be recognized.[3]

Noting the growing population of Oregon, he hoped that among those would come a "good sprinkling of industrious, thrifty colored people," who would be able to find jobs in Portland.[4] A year later, he voiced some complaints about the kind of black people that had come.

> We are sorry that the slums of the earth make Portland their homes, for they are making things very hard for our race here.[5]

Critical of any local activities that detracted from his image of black people, he commented on black participation in gambling and prostitution.

> If co-operative associations and business enterprises numbered among us as many as our pleasure clubs, we would be a more important factor in the commercial world.[6]

He also published many articles dealing with the growth of black-owned businesses and personal wealth, noting that the men at the Portland Hotel were saving money to buy houses. He also printed short biographies of black citizens, such as the following:

> The subject of this sketch scarcely needs any introduction at our hands to either the citizens or the traveling public; her name and fame extends to all parts of the country. Mrs. L. B. Lejeune was born in Rolla, Mo., she came to Oregon in "73, traveling by rail to San Francisco, thence to Portland by the *Ajax*, well remembered by all the old-time settlers. For twenty-three years she has kept a boarding house, and in 1884 in the advent of the transcontinental railroads to Portland she made a specialty of keeping a place where the railroad parties could call home. How well she has succeeded is shown by the fact that from that time to this her establishment is the leading one of its kind in the Northwest and the mention of her name carries with it a suggestion of something pertaining to the railway service.[7]

A. D. Griffin continued to publish the *New Age* until 1907, when he left Portland and moved to Louisville, Kentucky.

Portland's second black-owned newspaper, the *Advocate*, began publication in 1903.[8] It was founded by a number of local black men, including J. C. Logan, Edward Rutherford, E.D. Cannady, Howard Sproules, Edward Hunt, McCants Stewart, C. F. B. Moore, Bob Perry, W. H. Bolds and A. Ballard. E. D. Cannady served as editor, with the active assistance of Edward Ward, Sproules and Perry. Beatrice Cannady took an active role in the paper in 1912 when she became the assistant editor.

The *Advocate* was a four page weekly; national and local black news and black advertisements were printed on the front page, along with society news and entertainments of interest to the local black community. The second page contained national and state news of a general nature, and the fourth page was reserved for editorials, letters, church news, society news and hotel notes.

It was a more up-beat newspaper in philosophy than the *New Age*. While it did not hesitate to print examples of racial discrimination, it dealt in a positive way with the realities of black life in Oregon. Biographical articles featuring local black people and photographs of their businesses and homes were frequently published, and the newspaper was a valuable source of information for the black community during the thirty years of its publication.

Portland's third black newspaper, the *Portland Times*, was established in 1918 by W. R. Lee, William J. McLamore, J. D. Emery and E. R. Richardson. It ceased publication after five years, and very little of the paper has been preserved.[9]

The years between 1890 and 1914 saw the growth of agriculture, lumbering, fishing and industrial mining industries in Oregon, and produced great commercial expansion in Portland. The black press reflected this economic prosperity in its coverage of black enterprises, which were thriving.

> A visit to the several business enterprises being conducted by Negro men and women in this city would be in the nature of a discovery and agreeable surprise to the majority of our people and cause us to give up the belief that conditions are worse now than they were ten or twenty years ago. We find barber shops, grocery stores, restaurants, tailor shops, cafes, boarding and rooming houses, furniture stands, laundries, etc., all being run by Afro-Americans, and comparing favorably with any like establishments in the city.[10]

Most of the businesses served the needs of the black community, and many also represented second jobs for their owners. A black man named Horace Llewelyn Hubbard, employed as a mailing clerk and multigraph operator with the Underwriters Equitable Rating Bureau, conducted a dancing school with Mr. J. F. McClear. Owen L. Lynthecum was employed in Salem in the office of Governor Oswald West, had two residences in Portland, one in Salem, and a farm in Marion County.[11]

As black people were generally not permitted to eat in white-owned restaurants, black-owned restaurants and saloons provided a service to the black community and to railroad men away from home.[12] By far the most successful of these ventures was the Golden West Hotel. It furnished a place of residence for many of the railroad men, and also contained a restaurant, saloon, barber shop, ice cream parlor and candy shop. It was often used as a gathering place for the black community. One resident recalled these occasions:

> After church . . . we would go up to the hotel in order to have our dinner. Often they were swamped with customers all of a sudden every Sunday. So we utilized that time by visiting more with other people who had come out of other churches. There was a great swapping of . . . laughter, plans for the coming week, just a general get-together, socializing.[13]

From 1906 to 1931 the Golden West Hotel was operated under the management of a prominent black entrepreneur, W. D. Allen. In 1931 it closed for two years, and was reopened in November 1933, under the management of a black woman, Mrs. Catherine Byrd.

There were a number of people operating independent shops as barbers and hairdressers. James Fullilove managed a barber shop and was also a messenger for the U.S. District Court during the 1910s. Inez Mayberry was the first black woman to graduate from the Sanitary Beauty College in 1926, and for many years had a shop in her home near Mt. Tabor. Black men and women owned a number of tailor and dressmaker shops.[14] Edward W. and William H. Rutherford, who came from South Carolina in 1897 to work at the Portland Hotel, acquired property on Broadway and Flanders and for many years had a haberdashery, barber shop, cigar and confectionary store, and leased space for a café and tailor shop. Among the other businesses owned and operated by black people were grocery stores, butcher shops, transfer and storage operations, catering businesses, furniture dealers, auto repair shops, and a photography studio.[15]

The Enterprise Investment Company was established in 1901 by eight black men, who put up a capital investment of $10,000.[16] The organization bought land and erected a building on Larrabee Street, completing the project in 1903. The building was opened with a formal dance, the highlight of the season and the first, it was claimed, to be given west of Denver, Colorado, in a building owned by black people. By 1907 the value of the company's investments had increased to $13,500.[17]

The flurry of business activity in the black community which occurred in the first two decades of the twentieth century proved to be short-lived and by 1927 many of the businesses were no longer in existence. The *Advocate* assessed the progress of the black community that year, saying:

> We have three thousand colored people, and we are gradually increasing. For the most part we are buying our homes in all parts of the city. We have one large hotel, a newspaper, three modern barber shops, a confectionary, beauty parlor for the wealthy people, a branch YWCA, three churches and two missions. From the economic standpoint it is very difficult for one of our race to find other than menial work, yet we have two postal clerks, one shoe clerk, two stenographers in white offices, a clerk of the Child Labor Commission in the Court House, three men in the express business, one dentist and physician, and two attorneys.[18]

Employment opportunities for black people in private industry and government were largely limited to jobs as service personnel in hotels, restaurants, and in office buildings as janitors, doormen, porters, bellhops, waiters, and cooks. A.D. Griffin complained that while the black community had supported the Republican Party no "little jobs" were offered to black people. Later he reported that two political committees had hired black men; one as a clerk and one as a janitor.[19] One of the first black census enumerators hired in 1900 was M.W. Lewis. The first black mail carrier was Arthur A. Turner, who was hired in 1909 and remained on the job until his death four years later. A. Waterford was the first black man to work for the Portland Fire Department, and was appointed U.S. Deputy Marshall under Penumbra Kelly.[20] Ralph P. Flowers was employed by the city of Portland from 1919 to 1952 as an auto mechanic, and was the first black person to get a job with the city under the civil service program. At the time of his retirement he was in charge of the city municipal garage. He was also the first black person to operate a gasoline service station, and was the first to be issued a dealers license to sell automobiles. He operated a used car lot on Williams Avenue from 1939 to 1955.[21]

Employment for black women was also severely restricted. Meier and Frank Company hired black women as maids and Olds and King hired black women as elevator operators. Many were employed in private homes as domestic workers. Two women were employed as stenographers in offices, and Mrs. Lizzie Weeks was the first black woman to become a matron at the Frazier Detention Home and was appointed probation officer of the Juvenile Court by Judge Tazwell.[22]

The first black physician to practice in Portland in the twentieth century was J.A. Merriman, who came to the city in 1903. He remained in Portland until 1931. Dr. DeNorval Unthank, who was to become one of the most prominent black leaders of the community, came to Portland to begin his practice in 1930. Hugh A. Bell came to Portland to practice dentistry in 1924, and Dr. Elbert Booker, another dentist, came in 1927. McCants Stewart was the first black attorney in Portland, and was admitted to the Oregon Bar in 1903. In 1914 he ran for the office of public defender in Multnomah County, and lobbied for a public accommodations bill in the state legislature in 1919. Eugene Minor attended the Northwestern School of Law in Portland, and was admitted to the Bar in 1918. He practiced law in Portland for many years, and was also a librarian and messenger for the federal court under Charles E. Wolverton and Robert S. Bean.

The first black woman to practice law in Oregon, Beatrice Cannady also attended the Northwestern School of Law, and was admitted to the Oregon Bar in 1922.[a] In 1932 she ran for State Representative from District 5, Multnomah County, but was defeated. She moved to Los Angeles, California, in 1934.

a Beatrice Cannady did not pass the bar, but she was the first Black woman to earn a law degree in Oregon. See Kimberley Mangun, *A Force for Change: Beatrice Morrow Cannady and the Struggle for Civil Rights in Oregon, 1912–1936* (Corvallis, OSU Press, 2010).

Wyatt Williams worked for many years as a bellboy at the Portland Hotel and attended law school at night. In 1927 he was admitted to the Oregon Bar. He retained his job at the Portland Hotel, became captain of the bellboys, and practiced law in his spare time. He was employed as a legal assistant in the office of Julius Silverstone, and was also a real estate broker. In 1935 he worked as a courtesy attendant in the Oregon State House of Representatives.

Many of the young black people who grew up in Oregon in the 1920s and 1930s and who graduated from high school and college had to take menial jobs if they wanted to stay in Portland. There were few employment opportunities in the professions for educated black people. It was not until the 1940s that the first black school teachers were hired in Portland.

By 1941, the results of an industrial survey revealed that 98.6 percent of black people were employed in the railroad industry as waiters, cooks, porters, redcaps, and shop laborers. 0.1 percent were employed in private industry, and 0.4 percent in business and the professions.[23]

The railroad industry was always the most consistent employer of black workers. In 1931, when the Portland Hotel fired ten black waiters and replaced them with white waitresses, the men were hired by the railroad. Three months later, the Portland Hotel offered to re-hire the men and all but two went back. The two men who did not return to the Portland Hotel had found good jobs on the railroad and decided not to leave. Railroad jobs provided some degree of stability for the black community during the Depression, but the jobs came without any opportunity for advancement. Black men were confined to lower paying jobs and were not able to advance to positions traditionally held by white men. Wages were low and many men had to take a second job in order to support their families.

As early as 1900, black railroad men began to organize to improve working conditions; in 1912 Pullman porters from all over the United States presented petitions to the Pullman Company asking for an increase in wages. As a result, monthly wages were raised from $25.00 to $27.50. In 1917 another increase, to $45.00 a month, was secured. The Pullman car lines were placed under the U.S. Railroad Commission at the beginning of U.S. involvement in World War I. The commission only dealt with organized representatives of workers; the Pullman porters had no national organization. In 1918 they were granted the right of collective bargaining, and several organizations were formed to compete for the right to represent them. The Pullman Company took advantage of disunion among the porters, and in 1921 organized the Pullman Porters Benefit Association, using black "stooges" who went along with company policy, to ensure that all porters joined the union. Anyone refusing to join was fired.

In 1925 a rival union called the Brotherhood of Sleeping Car Porters was organized in New York City. It was considered a radical organization, because it was formed by the porters themselves, and because it addressed specific practices and working conditions it considered unfair. A porter was required to log 11,000 miles or work more than 400 hours a month before he would be eligible for overtime pay. Meals, uniforms, and supplies such as shoe polish had to be purchased out of the porter's salary. Porters had to "dead head," or report for work five or six hours ahead of the train's scheduled departure time, without pay, and remain at the station until the car to which they were assigned was full. They were also required to "double out," to come in off one train and take the next one out without rest, a chance to see their families, or shower and shave. If they appeared at the station tired or dirty, they could be suspended or fired. The porter in charge received only ten dollars a month more than the regular porters. The Pullman Company often replaced white car conductors who were paid $150 per month with black head porters who were paid much less. Black porters were also forced to put up with demeaning practices, to answer to the name "George," and to dance and clown for the passengers.[b]

A. Phillip Randolph, a former newspaper man and one of the founders of the Brotherhood, made extensive trips around the country organizing railroad men. By the end of 1926 local chapters of the Brotherhood were established in a number of cities, including Portland. It was an underground organization, as known membership could cost a man his job. The Brotherhood became the legal representative of the porters in 1935. In 1937 a reduction in work hours was secured, and wages were raised to $72.50 per month. A former railroad man and one of the organizers of the Brotherhood in Portland recalled the changes that the first contract brought.

> In all these years there had never been any such thing as a vacation, nor was there any such thing as having control over one's social life. After we got the contract all this was changed. In the years that followed, our salaries started moving up. And we began to have assignments which gave those with seniority the consideration due them.[24]

Between 1900 and 1940 the black population of Oregon increased from 1,186 to 2,565. The increase in actual numbers was slight, and in 1940 black people comprised only 0.24 percent of the total population of the state. Most lived in Portland, scattered in various parts of the city. In the absence of a large black population, life in Portland was often lonely for black people:

b Pullman porters were called "George" after George Pullman, founder of the Pullman Company.

> I can remember when we first came to Portland there was such a few colored people here that you'd go downtown and you wouldn't see another one . . . I used to walk to the railroad station and just sit . . . a couple of hours just to watch the colored waiters . . . just to see some colored faces.[25]

Local political, social, spiritual and fraternal organizations became the framework for the black community.

The social center of the black community before 1940 was in the black churches. Originally located on the west side, they began to move to the east side of the Willamette River following a general shift in population. One native black Oregonian recalled the importance of the black church as the center of social activity.

> The only time I came in contact with black people, and all of us did, was when we went to church. Because black people were scattered out over the city, and that was . . . the reason we went to church so much. That's the only time we got to see one another. As kids we'd go to Sunday School, and then your parents would come at 11:00 service, and then you'd go home, eat, then you'd come back, and after I got older I attended Christian Endeavor, and some of my friends who were Baptists they attended B.Y.P.U. And after Christian Endeavor was over, for those of us who could sneak away from church, we would go over to somebody's house and have what we used to call a "stomp." We'd have a crank up phonograph and we'd dance until 9:00.[26]

In 1923 there were five churches and two missions in the black community.[27] Musical programs were frequently presented, giving black musicians an opportunity to perform. Henri Le Bel, a theater organist in the days of the silent movie, was also organist for many years at the Bethel A.M.E. Church. Professor Elmer Bartlett, another organist, started the Bethel Negro Chorus. Over 100 men and women were members of this group. In 1932 they presented a series of concerts at the Multnomah Civic Stadium, called "Spirituals Under the Stars." Daniel G. Hill, minister of the Bethel A.M.E. Church in the early 1930s, also worked as a volunteer probation officer in the Multnomah County Department of Domestic Relations, and in 1932 compiled the first survey of black history in Oregon.[28]

The black church was outstanding in that it provided young people opportunities for participation and recognition not afforded in the public schools. Plays were presented; the Reverend J.J. Craw organized the performance of a number of the plays of William Shakespeare at the Bethel A.M.E. Church. Oratorial contests were held and birthdays and holidays were celebrated in style. The annual Sunday School Picnic was a big affair, attended by members of all the black churches. During the Rose Festival, the Mount Olivet Baptist Church had its own contest for queen, awarded to the woman who raised the most money selling tickets to a charitable event. A children's band was organized, and won prizes in the Junior Rose Festival parade.

Outside the black churches, the social life of the community was centered in the fraternal lodges and their women's auxiliaries, women's clubs, the Williams Avenue YWCA, and political organizations, the most important of which was the local chapter of the National Association for the Advancement of Colored People. These organizations all provided needed social, educational, political and charitable functions within the black community.

Masonic and Odd Fellows lodges were organized in Portland in 1883, and a black Elks lodge, the Rose City Lodge, was organized with its women's auxiliary, the Dahlia Temple, in 1906.[29] There was a local Knights of Pythias, the Syracuse Lodge, and in 1916 a second Elks lodge was organized.

These fraternal organizations provided important functions within the community. The Enterprise Lodge was composed of the more stable citizens of the black community; among other qualifications members had to be "free born," to pay their dues in cash, be of high moral character, and able to read and write. A lodge did not grant membership to transients; a man had to have a "settled abode" to be accepted. Dues collected provided for charity to the members, should they become sick or disabled, and for help to needy orphans and to the widows of deceased members. Lodges provided graves in the lodge cemetery plot, and conducted funeral services. They sponsored social events such as charity dances and excursions up the Willamette River, and helped to shape the moral standards of the community. It was an honor to be invited to join a fraternal order, and a person could be evicted for bad behavior or public drunkenness. Lodge sisters had to do charity work, and on a rotating schedule provided nursing care to members who were sick. This was particularly important as many black people did not have access to hospitals, and private nursing care was expensive and often unavailable.

In 1896 a conference was held in Boston, Massachusetts, attended by a group of black women in order to refute charges made by a white southern woman concerning the morality of black women. That meeting marked the beginning of an organization of black women's clubs to promote their common goals of self-education, high moral character, and the education of women and young girls. In 1897 the National Association of Colored Women's Clubs was formed, with the motto: "Lifting Others As We Rise."

A national conference of white women's clubs was called in 1902 to discuss integrating black and white clubs, and to allow black club members to attend national conferences with white women. Prior to this conference, each state's association of women's clubs voted on this proposal. Oregon's white club women voted to exclude black women's clubs, and the national conference, after much debate, also voted to continue the exclusion of black women from their organization and affiliated clubs.

In 1912 the Colored Women's Council was organized from a chapter of the Lucy Thurman Temperance Union. This group resolved to work for high ideals and morality, civic concerns and a Christian homelife.[30] In 1913 this organization held its first charity ball. A clubhouse was established in 1914, and the group joined the National Federation of Colored Women's Clubs. In 1917 nine Portland clubs organized the Oregon Federation of Colored Women's Clubs, to strengthen their organization and to unite to work for their common interests including betterment of the race and the education of black women and girls.

Club leaders were well-educated women and passed on what they knew to other women and girls. Like Girl Scouts and 4-H Clubs, they stressed arts and crafts, education, and community service. Funds were raised to provide scholarships for young girls, and the clubs participated in various political and social activities. During World War I many black women's clubs did volunteer war work. The Literary Research Club collected books and read and researched various topics of common interest, including a study of the laws of Oregon relating to minorities.

In 1921 a branch of the Portland YWCA was established in a portable structure on the corner of Williams and Tillamook Streets, and five years later work was begun on a new building on this site, funded primarily by a gift of $12,000 from a white woman active in the YWCA, Mrs. E. S. Collins. There was some opposition to the idea of a segregated facility, fueled by rumors that the gift, originally anonymous, came from the Ku Klux Klan. An effort was also made to deny the YWCA a building permit, prompted by white citizens who didn't want black people to build on the site. The protest was taken to the city council and the city attorney denied the request, saying that the city had no right to refuse to issue a building permit simply because it was for a black organization.

The idea of a segregated facility was not without its critics, but the Williams Avenue YWCA was managed by black women and became a community center. Many social and political clubs utilized the facilities of the YWCA for their meetings. The building had a gymnasium and auditorium with a stage, a kitchen, office, lounge, and locker rooms and showers for both boys and girls. Thirteen hundred dollars was raised by local black organizations to furnish the building. The YWCA had clubs for grade and high school girls. There were classes in Spanish, sewing, hat making, Bible studies, musical programs, dancing, games, exhibits featuring black artists, and activities celebrating Negro History Week.

Black people began to organize into political groups as early as 1870, when the Sumner Union Club was organized and endorsed the platform of the Union Republic party. It dissolved soon after, during a dispute over a local school board decision to prohibit black children from attending public schools. An organization called the Bed Rock Political Club was formed in the late 1870s, and was active until the waiters at the Portland Hotel organized the New Port Republican Club. This club had a membership of eighty, and was able to secure the employment of George Hardin, a black man, on the police force in 1894.[c] A chapter of the Afro-American League was organized in Portland in 1900, and in 1919 sponsored a civil rights bill which was presented to the state legislature.[31] The Colored Republican Club of Multnomah County was organized in the early years of the twentieth century, and in 1904 had a membership of 200.[32] In the 1930s two groups calling themselves the Colored Democratic League were organized.

A. D. Griffin was active in the Republican party, and was twice elected as a delegate to the state convention.[33] He was not always supportive of local Republican politics, and in 1902 complained that black voters were being ignored. He advised them to unite and cross party lines if necessary to elect candidates sympathetic to black interests.

> The *New Age* aims to be a progressive Republican paper . . . It is sincerely Republican in politics, on national issues, but locally the situation is so mixed just now that it is worthy of careful consideration and considerable study. So far as the Negro voters of Portland are concerned—some 800 of them altogether—The *New Age* thinks they should, on some proper occasion . . . show their power as a voting

c His employment may have begun sooner. On August 26, 1892, the *Oregonian* reported Hardin had been endorsed for office by an assembled group of Portland's Black community leaders. This group also endorsed the selection of Moody Scott of Ashland for a position as a clerk in the office of the Portland city auditor, which she received in September. See also Jacksonville *Democratic Times-Standard*, September 16, 1892.

> element in this community, and so call the attention of the Republican party leaders to the fact that they are alive, and have votes . . . the late Republican county and city convention forgot that there was such a thing as a colored voter. Out of 173 delegates not one colored face was there. It is now said that this was an oversight. Well, if the Negro should fail to vote for this or that or the other Republican candidate . . . it would not be an oversight . . . next time perhaps you won't forget that there are 800 Negro voters in this town—only remembering it on election day, when you need our votes . . . As long as there is so much independence in politics, the colored voter might as well begin . . . to be a little independent themselves.[34]

Despite Griffin's advice, it was difficult to maintain a unified political point of view. Political clubs were often divided as various candidates courted the black vote. It was not until the formation of the NAACP, with the support of a national organization and a national philosophy, that black people in Portland were able to organize successfully across political lines for the common good of the race. Even within this group, whose official position dictated that no political platform or candidate could be officially endorsed, efforts to secure the black vote created internal divisions from time to time.

The National Association for the Advancement of Colored People was created in 1909 from an interracial group, including W. E. B. DuBois, leader of the Niagara Movement. It was founded to work for an end to segregation and discrimination in housing, education, employment, voting rights and transportation, to fight racism and to secure full constitutional rights for black people. The Portland branch was organized in December 1914, with 165 members.[35] It was not the first western branch; chapters in Tacoma and Seattle, Washington, and northern California and Los Angeles had been established between 1912 and 1914. Dues were originally fifty cents per year, making membership within the reach of almost every person. Total membership fluctuated from year to year, and a good deal of local activity was given over to recruiting new members.[36] The most successful campaign before 1940 was conducted in 1928, organized by J. L. Caston, a young minister of the Mount Olivet Baptist Church. At the end of the year the total membership was 694.

Internal disputes threatened the organization's continuity several times during the 1920s. Mrs. E. D. Cannady, one of the original members of the branch and the most visible advocate for interracial understanding in Portland, criticized local blacks for a "do nothing" attitude.[37] She in turn was criticized for using the *Advocate* for her personal advancement, and only reporting NAACP activities in which she had a major role. Her criticism of the segregated Williams Avenue YWCA lost her the respect of many black people in Portland, although she remained a prominent advocate for black people in the white community. She organized branch chapters of the NAACP in Vernonia, Oregon, and Longview, Washington, and was appointed Branch Organizer for the national office. She was inactive in the local branch after 1929, although The *Advocate* continued to cover NAACP events and activities.

Attempts to buy the black vote also threatened to split the organization. In 1930, The *Advocate* reported the activities of the Political Committee, disrupted by the resignations of various members after Joe Keller, a white member of the committee, was rumored to have promised the entire black vote to one candidate for governor of the state. The *Advocate* reported:

> Mr. Keller cannot be blamed for his political aspirations, but it is the opinion of many that colored voters ought to be able to reach their own decision as to whom they care to support, without the aid of outsiders . . . when a candidate runs for office whose record is known of the Association to play politics, to be against Negro rights, the Association urges such a candidate's defeat . . . But the Association does not work for the election of candidates. This course seems to be the only wise one for such an organization to pursue, as it is a well-known fact that the Association is composed of both colored and white members representing every kind of political and religious affiliation. To play politics with the organization would soon wreck it upon the rocks of misunderstanding.[38]

Despite these internal disputes, the Portland branch is the oldest branch west of the Mississippi to be continuously chartered.

Much of the work of the local branch was given over to protest incidents of discrimination and to lobby for the passage of a public accommodations bill in the state legislature.[39] National black issues were also discussed, and charity events were held to raise money for the defense of black people involved in the criminal justice system. In 1925, a mass meeting was held to discuss the case of Dr. Sweet who, with ten other men, was in jail awaiting trial, charged with first degree murder in Detroit, Michigan. They were accused of killing two men who were part of a mob that was trying to drive Dr. Sweet and his family from their home. The *Advocate* commented:

> Shall these brave men who dared defend their home and the Doctor's wife hang for protecting their home and lives? Hear the answer at Mt. Olivet [Baptist Church] Monday night, Nov. 9th. This case specially

> concerns every colored man, woman and child in the United States, and every white man, woman and child who believe in the sanctity of the home.[40]

Between the Portland and Vernonia chapters, nearly $200 was collected for the Sweet Defense Fund. Clarence Darrow was hired to defend the black men, and they were acquitted.

Many nationally known individuals visited the Portland branch; the relatively isolated black community had first-hand access to national minority affairs. One such person was Leonidas Dyer, who visited Portland in 1923. The *Advocate* reported:

> Speaking before a representative audience at Lincoln High School auditorium Sunday afternoon, May 13, Congressman Leonidas C. Dyer, author of the famous Dyer Anti-Lynching Bill, made a lasting impression upon the minds and hearts of his hearers, when in plain unaffected language he told of the injustice to the race in this country . . . He took a fling at our Senators from Oregon and said that we should not forget their stand on this bill when they are up for re-election. He urged the people to join the NAACP, which he declared was the organization doing the most good and making the greatest and most effective fight for justice to the race.[41]

Educational and social events were frequently sponsored, such as one given in 1925 to acquaint the community with the black man Crispus Attucks, traditionally the first man to die in the American Revolutionary War. The *Advocate* announced:

> Under the auspices of the Portland branch of the [NAACP], a Crispus Attucks program will be rendered. This entertainment promises to eclipse all former ones in an effort to immortalize the name of the first martyr in the American Revolution, Crispus Attucks. The program will include such talented young matrons as Mrs. Zephra Baker, who will tell of Attucks the soldier; Mrs. Lulu Gragg, who will read a biography of Attucks. Mrs. Garner Grayson has been invited to give a brief sketch of her trip including her journey to the Attucks statue. J. A. Ewing, president, will tell the objective of the organization, and special music will be rendered.[42]

A women's auxiliary to the NAACP was organized in 1931 to coordinate fund raising activities. In 1931 and 1932, a Spring Carnival was organized, and in 1931 the group hosted a benefit card party to raise money for the

Scottsboro NAACP Defense Fund.

In 1933, conditions in Portland for black people were poor, as a news article reported:

> Unless something is done or some means found for employment, the outlook for many Negroes in Portland this winter is anything but encouraging. With many let out of the R.R. and hotel service, few are left with paying jobs. If it were not for the domestic service rendered by our women, it would be a tragic situation. The local branch of the NAACP held a timely meeting last Sunday upon the subject and it is hoped some definite program of procedure, beneficial to all will be worked out.[43]

During the Depression, the NAACP worked to secure employment for black people. Meetings were held in which speakers addressed the economic needs of black people, the need to acquaint employers with the situation of black unemployment, and to consider pooling black purchasing power. An organization called the Bureau of Economics was formed, to work toward opening an employment bureau, and to draft an employment campaign along the lines of the Urban League, which was not organized in Portland at the time. Two years later, although the Portland branch was having difficulty meeting its annual contribution to the national office, they were actively involved in arranging for black men to work on the Bonneville Dam Project.[44]

In the late 1930s, the local branch affiliated with the Oregon Commonwealth Federation, an organization of progressive liberals interested in minority rights. Although some people criticized the organization because they believed that it was too radical, the alliance resulted in positive change. Edgar Williams, local NAACP officer, commented:

> The only group of any political importance which has interested itself in our problems is the Oregon Commonwealth Federation. Within the year it has used its influence to place the first colored secretarial employees in the Federal and state offices in Portland, and is urging upon the school board the employment of at least one colored teacher . . . for the first time, due to O.C.F. endorsement, Negroes were elected to the Democratic county committee. At least 11 of the 15 Democratic legislative candidates, and about 7 out of 15 Republicans are pledged to support the Civil Rights Bill.[45]

In the first forty years of the twentieth century, blacks in Portland had solidified and expanded their community institutions, and were beginning to recover from the Depression, which had taken a harsh economic toll on the black community.

> They were like other people deprived of jobs. They hadn't any way to make a living, and we suffered too, because we were in that category. We were without work for well over a year. I did a number of things to help bring in money, and my husband worked for fifty cents a day shoveling snow down at the Hotel, and he would wear boots and walk from here to the Portland Hotel . . . in the snow up to his knees. People were just doing that. There were men with families who were going around with baskets of nuts and apples from office to office trying to make it.[46]

The accomplishments of the black community were achieved in the context of persistent discrimination, and the fight to achieve civil rights was passed from one generation to the next.

> I was told, "You've got to do better than the other fellow." I was told that you'd better stay in there and keep punching.[47]

George Washington, founder of Centralia Washington. Courtesy of the Oregon Historical Society Research Library.

Louis Southworth, ca. 1916. Courtesy of the Benton County Historical Society.

Mary Jane Holmes Shipley Drake, 1940. Courtesy of the Benton County Historical Society.

Richard A. and America Waldo Bogle. Courtesy of the Oregon Historical Society Research Library.

St. Paul's A.M.E. Church, Salem, Oregon, ca. 1892. Courtesy of the State Library of Oregon.

William "John" Livingstone. Courtesy of the Clackamas County Historical Society.

George Hardin, Portland's first Black policeman. Courtesy of the Oregon Historical Society Research Library.

Prospector believed to be Columbus Sewell, ca. 1860s. Courtesy of the Grant County Museum.

Union Station main entrance, Portland, 1913. Courtesy of the Oregon Historical Society Research Library.

Northern Pacific waiters, 1915. Courtesy of the Oregon Historical Society Research Library.

Portland Hotel, ca. 1916. Courtesy of the Oregon Historical Society Research Library.

Golden West Hotel. Courtesy of the Oregon Black History Project records.

Golden West Hotel candy shop. Courtesy of the Oregon Black History Project records.

W. D. Allen, founder of Golden West Hotel, 1919. Courtesy of the Oregon Historical Society Research Library.

J. A. Merriman, Portland's first Black doctor, 1919. Courtesy of the Oregon Historical Society Research Library.

Yearbook photo of McCants Stewart, 1899. Later the first Black person to practice law in Oregon. Courtesy of the University of Minnesota Archives.

Five members of the "Willamette Orchestra." Beatrice Morrow Cannady, second from right. Courtesy of the Oregon Historical Society Research Library.

Flowers family picnic, Portland. Courtesy of the Verdell Burdine and Otto G. Rutherford family collection, Portland State University Library.

Company 21, 116th Depot Brigade, nicknamed "The Portland Bunch," Camp Lewis, WA, 1918. Courtesy of the Oregon Historical Society Research Library.

View of Portland's Albina neighborhood, ca. 1900. Courtesy of the Oregon Historical Society Research Library.

Williams Avenue YWCA. Courtesy of the Oregon Black History Project records.

Tennis players at Mt. Scott, Portland, 1904. Courtesy of the Verdell Burdine and Otto G. Rutherford family collection, Portland State University Library.

Easter Sunday at Bethel A.M.E. Church, ca. 1913. Courtesy of the Oregon Black History Project records.

Cosmopolitan Club Ball, 1935. Courtesy of the Verdell Burdine and Otto G. Rutherford family collection, Portland State University Library.

8

A Very Prejudiced State

Discrimination in Oregon 1900–1940

Black people lived under discriminatory conditions in Oregon as well as in the rest of the nation. Social discrimination was common; black people were regularly refused admission to restaurants, theaters, and hotels. Medical care was difficult to obtain, unions barred blacks from membership, employment practices confined them to certain jobs and integrated housing was resisted. Passing a state public accommodations law to make discrimination illegal was a long and difficult struggle. It began in 1919 and despite repeated attempts was not successful until 1953.

According to a long-time black resident,

> Oregon was a Klan state . . . a southern state transplanted to the North . . . a hell-hole when I grew up. It has always been a very prejudiced state. It is today, believe it or not. There's a lot of prejudice even now, as far as that's concerned, but nothing like it used to be.[1]

The attitude of the black press changed, and contributed to greater activism within Portland's black community. A. D. Griffin, editor of the *New Age,* consistently maintained that prejudice was only confined to the lower elements of white society, and that the race problem would be solved when black people proved by their industry and good character that they were the equal of white people. The *Advocate* took a more positive position. Instead of elaborating on the problems of the black community, it focused the blame on white attitudes.

> Some white people are exceedingly generous with their advice to colored people as to how to solve the race problem in America. If these same individuals would take time to examine themselves, they would find that the key to the solution lay within. The race problem is not a one-sided affair: it has at least two sides like all other things. The white man is on the one side and the colored man on the other. Reading

history back three hundred years ago, we are constrained to believe the white man has the biggest side to solve . . . this white man is not willing to concede manhood, nor even human rights, to the colored man. When that individual becomes willing to deal justfully and manfully with his colored neighbor, then and only then will the race problem begin to be solved.[2]

Black people recall that many theaters practiced discrimination.

> I can remember my children going to the Egyptian Theatre on Union Avenue for years before we realized that the only place they could sit was in the balcony . . .[3]

In 1905 a decision by Judge Frazier in Portland set a precedent for the right of theaters to draw the color line. Oliver Taylor, a black man and Pullman car conductor, had purchased tickets for a performance at the Star Theatre but was refused seating by an usher who informed him that it was against the policy of the theater to allow black people to occupy box seats. The usher offered to exchange the tickets, but Mr. Taylor refused and sued the manager of the theater for $500 in damages. The judge ruled that a theater ticket is a revokable license, and that anyone could be refused admittance; the theater's only obligation was to refund the price of the ticket. This doctrine, the court said, applied to all people, and the fact that Mr. Taylor was black did not in any way influence the decision.

The *Oregonian* printed an editorial the following day which commented on the court's decision, agreeing with it based on the belief that theaters should respect the known prejudices of its patrons.

> If one person—a Chinaman, for example—has a right to buy any seat in the house, and sit in it, so may any other person—a Hottentot, or a woman of notorious reputation—do the same thing. It is not a question as to whether a white person objects to sitting next to a Chinaman. It is simply a well-known fact that he does object, and the theater must govern itself accordingly.[4]

The editorial concluded that the decision was probably good law, and clearly good sense.[a5]

---

a Taylor was represented by Oregon's first Black lawyer, McCants Stewart. The decision in *Taylor v. Cohn* was reversed on appeal to the Oregon Supreme Court in 1906, but racial discrimination in public accommodations was upheld in a nearly identical case eleven years later known as *Allen v. People's Amusement Park* (also argued by McCants Stewart on behalf of W. D. Allen). This case would preserve legal segregation in Oregon until the passage of the Oregon Civil Rights Bill of 1953. See Darrell Millner, "Blacks in Oregon," *Oregon Encyclopedia* (2021).

In the 1920s and 1930s the black community opposed discrimination by theater owners, and in some cases stood their ground and refused to be intimidated by theater managers and ushers. The *Advocate* commented when the Pantages Theatre, which made a practice of limiting blacks to particular seating, was robbed.

> Some local colored people think they see in the attack made on Jack Johnson, manager of the Pantages Theatre, by a holdup a few days ago, the unseen hand that, having hit moves on. Johnson may not have dealt a physical blow to a single colored person but he just as surely dealt and does deal the entire colored group a blow when he flatfootedly refuses them admission to his theatre in any part except the gallery.[6]

On one occasion Beatrice Cannady was able to obtain the seats she wanted for a show at the Oriental Theatre only after refusing repeatedly to take inferior seats. She related the incident in an editorial titled "Some of the Joys of Being Colored," where she described the incident and concluded:

> Guests see show but can't enjoy it because of the humiliation in obtaining seats.[7]

In 1929 a white lawyer, Milo C. King, persuaded the manager of the Pantages Theatre to give complimentary tickets to a black man and his children who were previously refused tickets, and the same year W. D. Allen and his son attended a performance at the Orpheum Theatre, ignoring the protests of the usher and manager. When the light went up at the end of the show Allen noticed that Chinese and Japanese were sitting in front and in back of him.[8]

In 1922 the license of R. D. Stuart, who operated a rooming house restaurant and cabaret at 220 N. 15th Street, was revoked, following a raid by police who observed white women dancing with black men. The action to revoke the license was taken by the Portland City Council under Mayor Baker, who declared, despite protests that racial intermingling was not unlawful, that there was one law that prevented it: the law of common decency. Baker instructed the council to draft an ordinance which would prevent racial intermingling in the future. He denied that race prejudice was a factor, saying:

> . . . when you take our white girls and allow them to get drunk in your establishment, and allow them to consort with negro men, I

want to say that it is humiliating to the white race and an insult to the decent negro people as well.[9]

Mr. Stuart said he had tried to keep the white trade out, but because of declining business was forced to let them come in. He said that he had not advertised his cabaret, and that white people had come in of their own free will. He also pointed out that city police frequently visited his establishment to evict intoxicated patrons, and they had assured him that he conducted his business in a satisfactory manner. Despite his protest, the decision to revoke his license was unanimous.

The black community and the NAACP sent a formal protest to the city council opposing the enactment of any discriminatory ordinance,

> . . . the language of which conveyed the impression that any colored people, regardless of their position in life, are lower than the lowest element of the white race, is not only a damaging statement to yourself and the white race, but is a direct insult to the colored people of this city.[10]

The black community objected to the passage of an ordinance prohibiting racial intermingling because it would set a precedent for discrimination already practiced in theaters and restaurants, and might lead to segregated streetcars, schools and colleges.

The city council decided an ordinance prohibiting racial intermingling would not be necessary, but supported Mayor Baker's decision to stop white women from dancing with black men in public in the interest of "common decency." The mayor hoped that his decision would have the support of the black community, saying,

> We can only assure those negroes who have signed their names to resolutions that they need have no fear of any action of the city council being taken to encourage in any way any race prejudice or anything against any law-abiding person of their race. We have found that no additional legislation is necessary and will handle the situation through police vigilance.[11]

Discrimination was practiced in restaurants, with or without the display of Jim Crow signs. It was the exception rather than the rule for white-owned restaurants in Portland to serve black people, as one resident recalled:

> I can remember the signs in all the eating places: "We Reserve the Right to Serve Whom We Please." I can remember around the corner

> a place called "Porky Pig," a hamburger place, my son and one of the boys who grew up next door to us going around there one evening to get a hamburger and being told, "Get out of here. We don't serve 'niggers' in here!"[12]

In 1907 the *New Age* noted that complaints of discrimination were increasing, where there had been little or no discrimination ten years before.

> It is within the memory of nearly all when Negroes' patronage was welcomed and largely sought for in such places as the Quelle and Freeman's, now they are excluded from both places and with this came a number of smaller fry following in the footsteps of the more stylish places.[13]

A. D. Griffin suggested that the actions of one black person, if dishonorable, reflected on the whole race, and attributed the increase in discrimination to the behavior of the local black community.

When the *Advocate* reported instances of discrimination, it suggested that black people boycott eating establishments that had refused to serve black people.

> It might be advisable for colored people who have been patronizing the Mannings' store to cease it. We have patronized the Mannings stores on 4th and Alder and also on Yamhill street for many years but from now on and until the Mannings stores cease to draw the color line, we shall find other stores in which to spend our money. Colored people must learn not only not to spend their money where they cannot work but also not to spend their money where they cannot eat.[14]

One incident that aroused the ire of the black community and the NAACP was a public announcement by a black man, Mr. B. J. Johnson, that his restaurant, The Barbecue, would no longer serve black people. The NAACP made a public announcement condemning Mr. Johnson. He quit his subscription to the *Advocate,* ten new subscriptions were obtained, and the restaurant soon went out of business.

The black community of Bend resented the use of Jim Crow signs and succeeded in having them removed. In 1925 a group of black men registered a protest with the Bend City Council.[b] They maintained that Jim Crow signs were a public humiliation to the black citizens of the town, who were

b According to Kelly Cannon-Miller of Deschutes County History Museum, this "group of black men" may have been just two persons—brothers Clarence and Earnest Phelps. The Phelps family represented most, if not all, of Bend's Black residents in 1925.

aware of which local restaurants would refuse to serve them. They said they had no desire to try to eat where they were not wanted, and preferred that owners refuse service to black people privately. The City Council adopted the resolution and had the signs removed.[15]

Jim Crow signs were also used in Portland. The *Advocate* reported one instance of their use.

> The Million Dollar Club Restaurant on Fourth Street, so we are told, has hung out a sign reading: we employ white help and cater to white trade. Heretofore this restaurant has served colored people as well as any other. However, colored folk can buy bread and doughnuts there to take home. But will they?[16]

NAACP monthly and annual reports mentioned success in having Jim Crow signs removed from various restaurants. One report stated,

> Nothing special outside of having signs removed from restaurants—"No Colored Trade Wanted."[17]

The Ku Klux Klan was reorganized in 1915, six months after the release of D. W. Griffith's film, *Birth of a Nation.* Based on Thomas Dixon's novel *The Clansman: A Historical Romance of the Ku Klux Klan,* this documentary style film claimed to present a true picture of the South during the Civil War and Reconstruction. It was sensationally and violently anti-black. The NAACP lobbied the National Board of Censorship, seeking the removal of some of the film's most obnoxious scenes, but that attempt failed, and the film was approved for public viewing. It then became the responsibility of local government to approve or deny permits to show the film.

In 1916 the film was scheduled to be shown in Portland. A group of black people, including Mrs. Katherine Gray, W. D. Allen, Rev. J. W. Anderson, Rev. R. W. Rowran, O. S. Thomas, E. D. Cannady, and representatives from the local NAACP, appeared before the city council to protest the showing of the film. The city attorney, council members, Mrs. Cannady, and other black citizens viewed the film, and the council passed an ordinance which would ban the showing of any film which would stir up hatred between the races.[18]

In 1922, James Weldon Johnson, National Secretary of the NAACP, sent a telegram to Ben Olcott, the governor of Oregon, to protest the showing of *Birth of a Nation,* scheduled to open at the Blue Mouse Theatre. Johnson urged Olcott to ban the film, saying,

> . . . we are informed that there are five hundred members of the Ku Klux Klan in Portland.[19]

The telegram was sent at the request of Mrs. Cannady. In 1923 the *Advocate* reported that the film was being shown in several theatres in Portland, " . . . but not a word of protest was heard from the local branch [NAACP]."[20]

The film was banned in Portland in 1926. In 1931, it was scheduled to be shown again, sponsored by the American Legion, who would receive a percentage of the profits for their charity work, and to raise money for a convention to be held in Portland the following year. Sound had been added to the film, and some of the more objectionable scenes were removed, but many groups joined the black community's protest, including the president of Reed College, the secretary of the Council of Churches, and several women's organizations. A private viewing of the film was held, attended by a large interracial group, who agreed that nothing substantial had been changed. The owner of the theatre withdrew his application to show the film. It was also cancelled in Salem because of that community's opposition.[21]

Although the Ku Klux Klan was organized in Oregon in 1921, groups of its type had existed in Oregon in the nineteenth century. Settlers coming from the border states and the South carried their baggage of prejudice with them: the activities of the Knights of the Golden Circle is only one example of the appearance of southern white-supremacy organizations in the West.[22]

Shortly after the turn of the century, an example of small town violence and southern style justice took place in Coos Bay, Oregon, then called Marshfield. The incident was reported in the *Oregon Journal:*

> Alonzo Tucker, the black fiend who assaulted the wife of Benjamin Dennis, at Marshfield yesterday, was captured and lynched by his pursuers this morning. Immediately after hearing the report that Mrs. Dennis, the wife of Benjamin Dennis, a miner, had been brutally assaulted by a negro yesterday afternoon, a party of men started in pursuit of the fiend and instituted a search that proved successful this morning. The frenzied men searched through the long hours of the night until early this morning the black fiend was discovered, who on seeing that he had been caught began to cringe and plead for mercy. He groveled in the dust, and clasped the knees of his captors crying with all his might for them not to hang him. But the hand of justice had secured too strong a grip on the miscreant and all the pleading in the world would not have saved him from the death he so thoroughly deserved.[23]

The *Oregonian* also reported the incident, using more restrained language. Alonzo Tucker was arrested the same day the crime was committed (neither newspaper questioned his guilt) and was placed in jail, escaping while officers attempted to move him to another jail. He spent the night under a wharf and was discovered the next morning. He was shot while trying to escape and died while being dragged to the scene of the crime. The rope was already around his neck, and his body was strung up over the south Marshfield bridge.

The body was cut down that afternoon and a brief inquest was conducted in the room where he had lived. The coroner's jury concluded that Tucker came to his death by a single rifle shot from an unknown person while resisting arrest and that no crime had been committed in his death. The newspaper article concluded:

> The conduct of the avengers was marked throughout by quiet orderliness but deadly determination. The sentiment of the community is in sympathy with the lynchers, and it is extremely improbable any arrests will be made.[24]

The *Oregonian* published two editorials concerning this incident, condemning the reporting style of the *Oregon Journal* article and the event itself.

> The correspondent . . . did not make a point for civilization nor yet for public safety when he spoke of the criminal as a "nigger" and declared him to be a "wild beast, to kill which was a duty." Prejudice of this type here presented is too narrow too wise in its own conceit, too utterly implacable, to be trusted in the jury room. In the community it is relatively harmless, since it does not in this day command the respect of any reasonable person.[25]

The editor pointed out that white men were serving time in the state penitentiary for committing the same crime and said that it was only "simple justice" that men who had committed the same crime be treated equally, regardless of race or color.

The second editorial was directed at a correspondent's attempt to justify the lynching because laws regarding assault were inadequate. The editor pointed out that in many southern states the penalty for assault was death, and yet the numbers of lynchings in these states were high. He deplored mob action, saying:

> Mobs murder prisoners not because they fear the law will not punish them, but because they enjoy the sport of murdering a wretch who has no friends. A mob is a coward, a brute and a fool . . . Mob murders are not due to the "inadequacy of the law" but to the desire of the mob to

> murder when it is safe to murder for the fun of it.[26]

The *Oregonian* was more interested in rhetoric than action; only the *New Age* suggested that some attempt be made to punish the lynchers so that a similar incident would not be repeated in Oregon.[27]

In 1924, another black resident of Marshfield, Timothy Pettis, was murdered. His mutilated body was found in the bay, and a $500 reward, plus another $100 put up by the local black community, was offered for the apprehension of the murderer. A telegram was sent from the Portland branch of the NAACP to the governor of Oregon, asking that a special investigator be assigned to the case. Lee C. Anderson also sent a letter to James Weldon Johnson, national officer, explaining the situation.

> Marshfield is infested with the Ku Klux Klan, and we are of the opinion, and so are the colored people who live in Marshfield, that all efforts are being made to cover up the crime. Colored people there demanded a second autopsy of the body which revealed that the testicles had been removed and it developed that it could not have been done except by [a] person or persons.[28]

The murder apparently remained unsolved; in the annual report for that year the Portland branch [of the Ku Klux Klan] wrote,

> The brutal murder of a colored man at Marshfield, Oregon was investigated by the organization . . . [it] gave us satisfaction in having accomplished our aim as far as physical power could act.[29]

The phenomenon of the Klan's rapid growth in Oregon in the early 1920s had little to do with local minorities: Catholics, Jews, Chinese, and blacks were few in number and there was little radicalism or labor unrest in the state. The nation as a whole had reverted to a new conservatism: the war had failed to eradicate communism, there were race and labor riots elsewhere in the nation, and a post war recession, increased immigration, and prohibition. It was an age of national paranoia, ripe for a movement that promised to restore law, order, and 100 percent Americanism to the nation.

The Klan's reign in Oregon was brief, but spectacular. It conducted an open anti-Catholic and anti-Jewish campaign. Membership estimates reached as high as 200,000, and the organization was able to influence the election of 1922 and to unseat its outspoken critic, Ben Olcott, the incumbent candidate for governor. The organization was also influential in securing the passage of a bill requiring compulsory public school attendance, which would have forced the closure of all private and parochial schools. This bill was passed but later ruled unconstitutional by a 1925 U.S. Supreme Court decision.

In January 1922, a Klan chapter was organized in Medford. Conditions favored the formation of a vigilante group: the chief of police was under heavy criticism from local churches and the W.C.T.U.[c] for failing to prosecute local moonshiners and bootleggers. One of the first acts of the Klan was against a black man named George Arthur Burr, a bootblack in Medford. He had been released after serving a three day sentence for bootlegging, and was picked up and taken into the mountains by members of the Klan. A rope was placed around his neck, and he was told to run. This "necktie party" was apparently a dress rehearsal for the Klan's next victim, a white man named J. H. Hale, a piano dealer and bond salesman. His offense was apparently initiating a lawsuit against a man who was a known Klan member. He too was taken into the mountains, a rope was placed around his neck, he was raised off the ground three times, and then ordered to leave the county or be killed. These two incidents, neither of which resulted in the victim's death occurred in March 1922. In April 1922, a second black man, Henry Johnson, a resident of Jacksonville, was treated in the same manner and ordered to leave town. A Grand Jury indicted six men in Jackson County on charges of riot and assault with a dangerous weapon. All of the persons charged (there were also sixteen "John Doe" indictments) were either acquitted or the charges against them dropped.[30]

Charles Maxwell, a black man and proprietor of a shoeshine shop in Salem, was threatened by the Klan in 1922. He received a letter, published later by the *Capital Journal,* that said:

> We have stood you as long as we intend to stand you, and you must unload, if you don't we will come to see you.[31]

The letter was signed "K.K.K." over a skull and crossbones. Charles Maxwell did not leave town, and in 1928 opened the "Fat Boy Barbecue" in the Hollywood district of Salem. His business was successful for a time, but after a bank foreclosure he moved to Los Angeles.

In Oregon City the following year, Perry Ellis, the only black resident of the town and the owner of a car wash, was nearly lynched by men thought to be members of the Klan. He had been accused of sleeping with a white woman, although charges against him were dropped when the woman failed to testify. He was called out of town, allegedly to pick up a team of horses

c Women's Christian Temperance Union

stranded on a country road with a broken down wagon. Ellis arrived at the scene with a white friend, Ira W. Thrall, to find two parked cars across the road. A spotlight was turned on Ellis, and six men appeared wearing masks. They ordered Thrall to return to Oregon City and drove Ellis about thirty miles out in the country, where he was interrogated and the men threatened to lynch him. He denied the charges concerning the white woman and they drove him to a lake where more threats followed. They finally let him go, ordering him to leave town or he would be killed.

Although both Ellis and Thrall were able to identify at least two of the men by their voices, no charges were brought, and Ellis left Oregon City for Tacoma, Washington.[32]

The Portland Branch of the NAACP sent a telegram to the governor of Oregon in 1921, protesting the appearance of the Ku Klux Klan in Oregon.

> The Portland branch of the [NAACP] representing more than three thousand colored people in the state of Oregon, and more than four hundred thousand colored and white members of the [NAACP] with headquarters in New York City, respectfully call your attention to the formation and rapidly spreading organization known as the Ku Klux Klan, under the pretense of promoters of law and order but aimed unquestionably at the persecution of individuals who may incur their disfavor. And to the end that all citizens may have a sense of security in their homes at night, and peaceable protection in their places of business and employment during the day, we humbly pray your honor to prevent in our State, any organization or public demonstration of the said notorious [K.K.K.] under any pretext whatsoever.[33]

The same year a mass meeting of black people was held and appointed a committee to visit the mayor of Portland to protest a Ku Klux Klan street parade.[34] The Klan paid a visit to the Reverend Moses Riley, a Portland minister, threatening him because white people attended his church and were seen going in and out of his home. There were other threats involving black families who were moving into white neighborhoods, but the black community was armed and prepared for the Klan, and protected individuals whose property was threatened.[35]

In 1903 an attempt was made to integrate the public schools of Coos Bay. Three black children tried to attend school but were refused admission by the principal. The school board directed him to provide a separate room where the black children could be taught, to hire a teacher, and insure, as the *New Age* reported,

> . . . that equal school privileges are provided for said Negro children as are now enjoyed by the white children of this district.[36]

Editor Griffin predicted that the taxpayers of Coos County would not long stand for the extra expense of the separate school.[d]

School segregation existed in the 1920s in Vernonia and Maxville, and also in Catholic schools in Portland. The black people of Vernonia had come from the South as employees of the Oregon-American Lumber Company, and their presence caused some concern in this small settlement in the Coast Range some thirty-five miles northwest of Portland. Initially, there were only five black children of school age, and as the local school would not admit them, they had to attend school in Portland. The local school district tried to set up a segregated school in a shack, but Mrs. Beatrice Cannady went to Vernonia to intercede for the black children and in 1926, one year after the black people arrived in town, their children were admitted to the public schools. One local resident, who taught in the Vernonia school in 1927, recalled that a real attempt was made to ensure that the black students received fair treatment.

> I had about five Negro children in first grade. One was a typical little black girl named Katie. One day as the class lined up to march in from recess she gave a healthy push to a white child and I pulled her out of line. When I asked her why she had done it, she replied: "My Mama told me not to let any old white trash push me around, and he pushed me!" I informed her we were all equals in this school and we had no trash—white or black—and told her not to do that again . . . I do recall that one black boy became student body president one year and they participated in May Day activities and marched with the white students at graduation. Here, they were people on a par with everyone else.[37]

The situation in Maxville, a small town near La Grande in eastern Oregon, was similar. Bowman Hicks Lumber Company had brought people from the South, both white and black, to work in the lumber mill. In 1926 Mrs. Cannady received a letter from J. L. Stewart of La Grande describing the

d A school for colored children in Marshfield operated on and off until 1911, serving Black and Chinese students. The school was formed in response to Lily Trollinger's petitions to allow her four children admission into the local school. In 1903, school superintendent Franklin Golden denied her request, stating, "On account of the physical condition of said Negro children and their lack of cleanliness, their presence in the white classes will materially retard the progress of the three hundred thirty white children now in attendance." See Jon Littlefield, *Between Two Worlds: Chinese of Marshfield*, Oregon, 2012.

situation. The black children were not allowed to go to school during the daytime, but were taught instead by a black woman in her home. Mrs. Cannady advised the residents not to accept a segregated school, even if it meant teaching the children at home. Ellen Law lived in Maxville as a child, and attended a public school in the nearby town of Enterprise. Her father and mother had moved to Oregon from Arkansas, hoping to find better conditions, only to discover that they were the same or worse in Oregon.[38]

Catholic schools in Portland were briefly segregated: in 1926 the *Advocate* printed a harsh editorial condemning segregation in parochial schools. The article was titled "The K.K.K. and the Katholics," and pointed out that in two recent attempts to enroll black children in Catholic schools in Vancouver, Washington, and Portland, the children were denied admission because they were black. The *Advocate* wondered if it had been wise to urge its readers to vote to support parochial schools, since the Catholics, as well as the K.K.K., seemed to be hostile to black people. The article concluded:

> We admit that we are puzzled over the thing and wonder if it is true that the policy of the Catholic Church is to draw the color line.[39]

In the 1930s St. Mary's and St. Andrew's Catholic Schools in Portland admitted black children.[40] In the NAACP annual report for 1939, three school cases of prejudice were reported: a suspension of a student was settled satisfactorily, a teacher who called a black child "nigger," and another teacher who said Marian Anderson was a communist and apologized after the NAACP intervened.[41]

Black Portlanders recalled the difficulties of buying a home:

> When we bought this place . . . the neighbors had a petition for us not to buy the place. But we did have a black neighbor across the street, and to the side of us. But they didn't want any more in here.[42]

In the 1920s and 1930s segregated housing patterns began to form in Portland, and opposition to black people buying homes or renting apartments in white neighborhoods became more vocal. Until this time, black people lived and bought homes in all parts of the city. If necessary, realtors were bypassed and housing was secured by using a white attorney as a go-between.

In 1919 the Portland Realty Board added to its code of ethics a provision prohibiting its members from selling property in white neighborhoods to blacks or Orientals, because they believed that such sales tended to cause a drop in property values.[e][43] In 1930, Dr. DeNorval Unthank moved into a suite in the Panama Building, where Dr. E. L. Booker, another black man, had been practicing dentistry for three years. Because of tenant opposition, Dr. Unthank was forced to find office space elsewhere, and moved his medical practice to the Commonwealth Building at 5th and Burnside Streets.

The same year an article in the *Advocate* predicted that if the black community was not careful it would find itself confined to an area around Williams Avenue, and pointed out the consequences.

> We all know what residential segregation means. It means poor housing, bad streets, and if the streets are paved, poorly kept; deficient lighting. It also means separate schools and their attendant shortcomings. It invites race riots, because the stronger race will feel that the weaker has no rights outside of its restricted district and any attempt on the part of the weaker to exercise its rights of liberty, at all, is met with opposition from the stronger; the trouble begins. It is segregation that is the root of all interracial troubles. We think that many of us will live to see Portland the spectacle of separate schools and all the rest of the segregation as practiced now in the South. It is reasonable to expect it in the wake of residential segregation and colored people, some wittingly and others unwittingly, are hastening this condition in Portland. If we could convince ourselves that there will be no such thing as world peace, then we would not lift our voice against the segregation of the races.[44]

In 1930 Dr. Unthank and his wife moved into Ladd's Addition, an exclusively white neighborhood.[f] They had been forced to move four times previously because of racist opposition. Visited by a group of citizens, they were informed of a petition signed by seventy-five people objecting to their presence in the neighborhood. Among those who paid them a visit were two school teachers. The house was vandalized, windows were broken and

e On March 2, 1919, the *Oregon Journal* reported this resolution was unanimously recommended; however, the March 6 article cited here reports that the provision still needed to be approved at the Portland Realty Board meeting the following day to go into effect. The next day, the journal reported that the motion failed, writing, "After considerable debate this morning the Portland Realty board, at a meeting of its members in the Benson hotel, laid aside the motion prohibiting the sale of property to orientals and negroes indefinitely."

f Subsequent research has determined that the house the Unthanks bought was in Westmoreland, not Ladd's Addition, in 1931. The *Oregonian* reported that a committee from the Westmoreland Protective League met with the Unthanks in an effort to persuade them to leave the neighborhood with offers of cash for their equity and moving expenses, an offer the Unthanks refused. While negotiations went on inside the Unthank's residence, a mob of fifty residents gathered outside, and police had to be called to disburse them. See the *Oregonian*, April 30, 1931, and July 11, 1931. Thanks to John Mead, former director, Reference and Research Collections, Oregon Historical Society, for correcting this error.

garbage and even a dead cat were thrown on their lawn. The Unthanks cleaned up the mess, repaired the windows, and a few months later they were broken again. His wife accused their neighbors, Mr. and Mrs. Fred Jones, of vandalizing their home and Mrs. Unthank was charged with threat to commit a felony. The charges against her were eventually dropped, and the Unthanks moved from the neighborhood.

In 1932 the Rose City Company brought a suit against Mrs. Ida Tindall, seeking to remove her from a house which she had bought in a white neighborhood. The practices continued; in 1949 a man was expelled from the Portland Realty Board for selling property to a black man in a white district. In the annual report for 1939, the local branch of the NAACP made this comment:

> Still working on real estate boards discrimination to colored home buyers. They take down payment, let them clean house and then say sorry they cannot let them live there. Because a neighbor complained. Investigation says neighbor is usually blocks away.[45]

The University of Oregon refused to allow black women to room in the college dorms with white women. Maxine Maxwell of Salem enrolled in the school in 1929, and had to live twelve blocks from campus with another black girl, Miss Franklin.[g46] This practice continued into the 1930s and 1940s. Ellen Torrance Law recalled her days at the University of Oregon, living in a basement room with only cold running water, stoking furnaces to pay the rent, because she was denied a room in the college dormitories.[47]

When blacks moved to Portland, they found that job discrimination was widely practiced:

> There weren't any good jobs. The only jobs here in Portland at the time we came here was if you didn't railroad, the Portland Hotel, and the women [had maid work] at Meier and Franks, and the barbershops . . . there weren't any good jobs.[48]

When the local Laundry Workers Union refused to open their membership to black women, A.D. Griffin commented that this was worse than in the South, where black people who worked in menial jobs were protected. He

g This discrimination existed even earlier. University of Oregon's first Black student, Mabel Byrd, had to reside in the off-campus home of history professor Joseph Schafer, and worked as the Schafer family's domestic servant while attending school in 1917. See University of Oregon Special Collections & University Archives "Unbound" blog, February 4, 2015.

also pointed out that the local Teamsters Union and Cooks and Waiters Union refused to allow black people to join. He predicted that in the end black people would be admitted to these unions, but in the meantime,

> . . . as long as the Unions discriminate against our people, let us show them that they cannot expect our help or sympathy. Let us call the attention of all our friends to their attitude toward us and in the end they will be compelled to grant us our rights.[49]

Griffin later approved of a man who obtained work as a truck driver for the Banfield, Veysey Fuel Co., whose regular drivers were on strike, and suggested that other black men seek work in similar situations.

> We have repeatedly warned [the Unions] that . . . in case of a strike or difference between them and their employers the Negro would have no cause to feel any pangs of conscience about taking the place of the strikers.[50]

When the Civil Service and Police Commission ruled that no one who had worked as a janitor or porter in a saloon could qualify for a position on the police force, Griffin wondered if the same rule would be applied to white applicants, and concluded:

> Shut out by the Unions, who refuse to admit the black worker to membership, from securing more lucrative employment, the fact that he accepts menial labor rather than steal or starve, in the eyes of our Democratic commissioners counts against him. Verily where an excuse is wanted, it is not hard to find one.[51]

In 1924, the *Advocate* reported that white waiters were hired in the Portland Hotel's grille room, because the unions insisted that these jobs should not be given to black waiters.[52] The NAACP intervened when black employees were discharged by Olds and King, and they succeeded in having the women rehired. A new position was also created and filled by a black man. They were able to make small gains with other employers, but discrimination in employment continued, and black people were generally barred from unions until 1949, when the Oregon Legislature passed a fair employment practices act, making discrimination in employment illegal.[53]

In the years before World War II, discrimination was persistent, but not as intense as that which was experienced during the 1940s. One resident recalled,

> It seems that most black people thought that we didn't need a civil rights law, because they could go wherever they wanted, and participate in anything they wanted, and buy wherever they wanted. But when the war came along and a lot of blacks came in from different states, that's when they started discriminating. So blacks found out that they needed a civil rights law.[54]

The degree of discrimination that black people experienced varied from person to person and place to place. The most extreme examples occurred in small towns such as Coos Bay and Medford, where the Ku Klux Klan was strong. Black people in Portland faced continued inequalities in employment, housing, and public accommodations.

An active leadership developed that protested incidents of discrimination, often successfully. But the power of the black community was limited and operated without civil rights legislation and a large population that could initiate economic boycotts and exert political pressure. Many black people were leaving Oregon. In 1936, for example, the black population of Salem had virtually disappeared, as a local NAACP officer observed:

> Salem has no Negro population, except a few inmates in the Penal Institution, and Insane Hospital. All of the colored people who did live here, have all moved to Los Angeles. I know of no Negro living in Salem at the present time.[55]

As one resident remembered, a good deal of energy had to be spent simply in making a living.

> We were just a mere handful of people here in Portland . . . We were so scattered. We had people living as far as Lents, St. Johns, and heck, you couldn't get them together! Then on top of that the majority of men were railroad men. They were out of town.[56]

9

Simple Justice

Civil Rights Legislation 1893–1939

Black people began to go to the state legislature as early as 1893, lobbying to repeal the defunct sections of the state constitution that excluded blacks and Chinese from the state and prevented them from voting, and also to repeal the ban on intermarriage and pass a public accommodations law. Despite repeated efforts, the only successes before 1940 were the repeal of the exclusion clause and the ban on voting, clauses which had been inoperative since the Civil War.

Having no representatives in the state legislature, black people had to rely on white legislators willing to introduce bills on their behalf, on lobbying efforts and by uniting in political groups and coalitions that voiced the collective needs of the black community. This took place in a time when many black men were employed on the railroad and often out of town, or working in menial jobs, struggling to provide their families with the necessities of life; much of the work was carried out by a handful of people, as unpaid volunteers.

Oregonians have historically maintained an attitude of hostility to outsiders and minorities. The framers of the state constitution relied heavily on the constitutions of midwestern states, especially that of Indiana, but came up with some original clauses that had no precedent. It is striking that all of the important sections relating to the rights of minorities were in this category.[1]

The original procedure for amending the constitution was lengthy and complicated, requiring approval by two successive legislatures and then referral to a general election. This procedure was modified in 1906, when only one legislative endorsement was required and any amendment had to be submitted to the voters at the *next* regular or special election. No amendments to the constitution were approved before 1902, when the Initiative and Referendum amendment was passed. Between 1902 and 1926, when the exclusion clause was finally deleted, nearly fifty amendments to the constitution were approved.

In the 1891 legislative session, some thought was given to amending the constitution or to creating an entirely new one. A resolution to call a constitutional convention was introduced, as

> . . . it is the opinion of a large portion of our citizens that the constitution of Oregon is in many respects repugnant to the changed condition of affairs since that instrument was adopted . . .[2]

In this and the next assembly resolutions were introduced which would give the legislative assembly the power to pass registration laws to regulate voting rights; both failed to gain majority approval.

A flurry of constitutional amendments were introduced in the 1893 session, among them three designed to correct the constitutional exclusion of blacks and Chinese, and the ban on voting. This campaign was initiated by members of Portland's black community, who met in January 1893 to organize the campaign. Resolutions were introduced in the legislature by Representative Henry H. Northup of Multnomah County, at the request of the Reverend T. Brown, pastor of the First A.M.E. Zion Church of Portland, the spokesman for the black community. All three resolutions were approved with little or no opposition.

The resolutions were re-introduced in the 1895 session, where only the repeal of the exclusion clause was approved. The special act required to submit amendments to a general election was overlooked in the final days of the session, so this amendment was not submitted at the next general election. The 1897 session was involved in political disputes, the House did not even organize, and it was left to the 1899 session to pass the necessary enabling bill. Finally, in 1900, the repeal of the exclusion clause was submitted to the voters.

The attitude of the press toward modifying the constitution was initially favorable. Both the *Oregonian* and the *Oregon Statesman* approved the actions of the 1893 legislature, the later calling their actions a "Great Awakening," predicting that other amendments to the constitution would soon be approved.[3]

The most controversial of the five amendments submitted to the voters in 1900 was a proposal allowing women to vote. The other amendments, beside the repeal of the exclusion clause, dealt with municipal indebtedness, the judicial system, and irrigation. The *Oregonian* printed several articles prior to election day which predicted the defeat of all of the amendments.

> It is not necessary to amend the constitution of Oregon. It is good enough and better than would be made or could be made now . . . The more we amend it the more likely we are to worsen it.[4]

The *Oregonian* particularly encouraged its readers to vote against women's suffrage.

Many voters, however, ignored the amendments entirely, and did not cast a vote on them. All of the amendments were defeated; the amendment to repeal the exclusion clause received the smallest number of votes. Defeat was by a painfully small margin.[5]

In an editorial published shortly after the election, the *New Age* speculated that the measure was defeated because Oregonians felt that the state constitution was superior to the federal constitution.

> The result of the vote on repealing the section in the constitution placing restrictions on the rights of Negroes and Mulattoes in the matter of residence and the holding of property in this state showed a woeful lack of intelligence on the part of a majority of the voters when they voted against the repealing of that section for admitting, as *The Oregonian* claims, that it is abrogated by the action of Congress in passing the 14th amendment of the constitution. There are still those who claim that the state is superior to the United States and if the question was ever brought to an issue would uphold the constitution of the state I preference to the constitution of the United States. And while we do not fear that this country would . . . allow such a view to stand, still it is better to have nothing in the way of a clear understanding of our rights and duties as citizens of this state.[6]

Other resolutions to repeal the exclusion clause were passed in 1901 and 1903, without opposition. The *New Age* predicted that if the amendment was presented to the voters again it would be easily approved, calling the exclusion clause "a relic of ante-bellum, pro-slavery prejudice, that should be expurged from our organic law."[7]

Such was not to be the case for many years; although the amendment was twice approved in the legislature, no enabling bill was passed and it was not included in subsequent elections.

Between 1905 and 1915, the issue of minority rights was virtually forgotten at the legislative level. Two curious bills were introduced in 1909, both "by request." One proposed to ban Chinese from practicing medicine, and the other to ban Chinese gambling games. Both were defeated.

In 1915 a novel solution to repeal the exclusion clause was proposed by Representative D.C. Lewis of St. Johns. His bill would simply prohibit the *printing* of that section as part of the constitution. This bill was indefinitely postponed, and suffered the same fate when it was introduced in the 1917 session.

Attempts to repeal the exclusion clause were dropped for the next seven years. In 1925, a bill to repeal the exclusion clause was introduced by William F. Woodward, Republican from Multnomah County, at the request of a black woman, Mrs. Lenora Freeman, and a delegation from the League of Women Voters of Portland.[8] Woodward, a political maverick, had accepted the support of the K.K.K. in his campaign for election to the state legislature of 1923.[9] This bill authorized the Secretary of State to set aside two pages in the Voter's Pamphlet for publication of arguments in support of the measure, and to appoint a committee of three legislators to prepare the arguments. It passed easily in both houses, receiving only one negative vote.

The argument prepared and printed in the Voter's Pamphlet traced the history of the exclusion clause, its nullification by the Fourteenth Amendment, and earlier attempts to remove it from the constitution. It was characterized as:

> a constant reminder of intolerance and hatred, a reproach to the people of the commonwealth, a slur upon those whom it sought to proscribe . . . Vote for this repeal and thus uphold the spirit of Abraham Lincoln—The great Emancipator.[10]

Repeal was also urged for the sake of school children who were expected to study and obey the constitution.

The *Oregonian*, which for years had been opposed to widespread modification of the constitution, was critical of the number of amendments submitted that year, nineteen in all. Its readers were advised, "When in doubt, vote NO."[11] In a later article its recommendation on the exclusion clause amendment was reversed, and approval was urged because it corrected "an absurdity in the Constitution."[12] Other newspapers either endorsed the measure half-heartedly, or published lengthy articles about the history of the exclusion clause in an attempt to provide an explanation for its original inclusion in the constitution. In some cases voter ignorance and racism was cited as the cause for previous defeats. It was an easy opportunity to denounce intolerance and racism, as the amendment had no public opposition.

The *Advocate* published restrained articles favoring repeal, and speculated that previous failures to repeal the clause were due to "ignorance of the real status of the Negro in the State."[13] The paper urged black people to register and vote to support the measure, reminding them that blacks in the South were denied the right to vote.

The final vote was 108,332 in favor, 64,954 opposed. 26 percent of those who voted, more than 60,000 people, did not cast a vote on the amendment.[14] The *Advocate* reproached those who had voted against the amendment as being either very ignorant or very prejudiced, and wondered why, in the Republican state of Oregon, the clause had not been repealed sooner.[15]

The first attempt to repeal the ban on voting occurred in the legislative session of 1893, although the bill was worded to repeal another section.[16] The resolution was approved in 1893, but defeated in the 1895 session. No attempt was made to repeal the ban on voting again until 1915, when Senator McBride proposed an amendment at the request of the black community, and specifically by McCants Stewart, a black attorney.[17] The resolution passed easily in both chambers, receiving only two negative votes. The amendment came before the voters in the election of 1916. The Voter's Pamphlet reprinted the full text of the resolution, and also the text of the section to be deleted from the constitution. It said in addition that it was "an amendment to the Constitution of the State of Oregon removing the discrimination against negro and mulatto citizens."[18] The article did not point out that the section had been nullified by the Fifteenth Amendment, and no arguments in support of the measure were printed.

The press in general either ignored the amendment or favored repeal because it was obsolete and an embarrassment to the state. The *Oregonian* printed a short endorsement the day before the election:

> It is a matter of history which we would fain forget that the state of Oregon was one of six states to reject the Fifteenth Amendment to the United States Constitution. There is an opportunity this year for Oregon to retrieve its record. There is up for passage an amendment repealing the now inoperative section of the state constitution denying the right of suffrage to negroes and mulattoes. The presence of the section in the constitution is an unpleasant reminder.[19]

The final vote was close: 100,027 voted for repeal, 100,701 against. This represented 75 percent of the total number of voters: 25 percent did not vote at all on the issue. A majority in every county except Multnomah, Benton, Washington, and Yamhill voted against repeal.

The *Oregon Voter*, a non-partisan political paper which had favored the amendment, ascribed defeat to race prejudice, and admitted that voter ignorance was also a factor.

> Ignorance there was, no doubt, but the race prejudice was reflected nevertheless, and to our knowledge many voted "NO" in a spirit of protest, realizing full well that the vote could have no effect on the citizenship status of the negro.[20]

In the opening days of the session of 1927, Representative John Geisy of Salem submitted another resolution to repeal the ban on voting. Space in the Voter's Pamphlet was to be provided for arguments in support of repeal, and the actual wording on the ballot was to include a statement noting that the clause was in conflict with the federal Constitution, and repeal was necessary to complete the removal of obsolete, racist clauses. His resolution was approved, and the repeal amendment again came before the voters.

The press was restrained in its attitude toward the amendment, viewing it as an afterthought. The *Advocate* issued only one brief statement in its pre-election issue, saying the clause was ". . . a disgrace to [Oregon's] fair name."[21]

The amendment was approved, although by a smaller margin than the vote to repeal the exclusion clause the year before. The final tally was 69,373 in favor, 41,887 opposed.

Before 1940, two attempts were made to repeal the state law banning intermarriage. In 1893, a bill was initiated by a black minister, the Reverend T. Brown, who stayed to lobby for the bill throughout the session. The bill was voted down in the Senate, where it had been introduced by O. N. Denny, from Multnomah County. The *Oregonian* reported that the reason for defeat was that the children of mixed marriages "retain all the vices of the parent, and do not associate with either whites or negroes."[22]

The only Senator to defend the bill was H. E. McGinn, from Multnomah County, who argued that black people should not be deprived of their rights and privileges "simply because that at the building of the tower of Babel some went in one way with black skins and other in another with white [skins]."[23] McGinn was a colorful figure in the politics of that era. In his early years he publicly supported vice and gambling operations, and participated in them himself. As a modern historian noted,

> He loved booze and women and was not afraid to admit it. Paradoxically, his voice carried authority in a community that ostensibly disdained such activities.[24]

He later repented of the corrupt practices of the 1890s and early 1900s, when bribery on election day secured the victory of the party machine candidates. He died in the 1930s in his favorite brothel, and was mourned by Portland's elite.

The bill to permit intermarriage introduced in 1893 was also defeated in the Senate, by a vote of nine in favor, and twenty opposed. The proximity of this bill with others that were approved which would remove the obsolete sections of the state constitution indicated how far the legislature was willing to go on behalf of the rights of black people and other minorities. Clearly, it was acceptable to modify the state constitution in order to affirm rights guaranteed by the federal Constitution, but the legislators of Oregon were not ready to grant additional rights to minorities, including the right to marry whom they pleased.

In 1911 a curious bill on the subject of intermarriage was introduced. This bill would have added to the list of prohibited unions those between whites and Hindus or Japanese. This bill found its way to the legislative scrap heap, and a vote was never taken.

In the 1917 legislative session, D. C. Lewis, Republican from Multnomah County, introduced a bill in the house that would have allowed intermarriage.[25] He defended his bill, saying, "if a white man loves a colored woman or a Chinese woman, let him marry her."[26] The *Oregonian* recommended that the bill be defeated, saying: "It is not in line with the movement for uplift of the colored race."[27] The bill was referred to the Committee on Health and Public Morals, where it was returned to the House with the recommendation that it be defeated. The House accepted the committee's recommendation, and the bill was defeated without a vote.

Before 1940, the black community did not again lobby to remove the ban on intermarriage, concentrating instead on efforts to pass a public accommodations bill. Vancouver was just across the river, and interracial marriages were not prohibited in the state of Washington.

In 1919 the Afro-American League of Portland drafted the first civil rights bill to be presented to the state legislature, persuading John B. Coffey, Republican member of the House from Multnomah County, to introduce it. The bill, called "an act establishing equal rights in places of public amusement," guaranteed to all citizens equal enjoyment of public accommodations and prohibited the printing or posting of signs indicating that service would be refused to anyone on the basis of race or color.[28] The bill included a lengthy list defining places of public accommodation, which covered virtually every kind of commercial establishment except private clubs. The penalty for violation of the law was a fine and/or a jail sentence.

The bill was originally referred to the Multnomah Delegation, who returned it with the request that it be sent to the Committee on Health and

Public Morals.[29] In this committee the bill survived various attempts to bury it. Republican D. C. Lewis wanted to have the bill delayed until the last day of the session, where it would be caught in the rush of last minute business and forgotten. This bill and two others were stolen from the committee chairman's desk, and new bills had to be drafted from the printed copies. The committee heard arguments in favor of the bill from Rev. W. L. Rowan, Micco T. Harjo, and Mrs. E. D. Cannady.[a]

The bill was reported back to the House without recommendation, where it provided, in the words of an *Oregon Journal* reporter, "an hour and a half of excitement, mixed with a considerable amount of levity, before being finally killed."[30]

After the bill was read, a member moved for indefinite postponement. His motion was followed by a chorus of "ayes" and as the Speaker of the House was about to announce the bill's death, Representative Eugene E. Smith of Multnomah County objected, requesting the legislature to give some consideration to the black voters who had initiated the bill, who were the same voters the Republicans loved to brag about at election time. Smith was the bill's only defender.

Mrs. Alexander Thompson, a Democrat from The Dalles, said that she would vote against the bill because she was a Southerner, but no Republican could oppose it and be consistent with the party's historical attitude toward Reconstruction. Her chiding was sufficient to defeat a move for indefinite postponement, and the bill came up for a third reading, and a vote. As several members of the House were absent, a roll call was requested and taken, and D. C. Lewis was missing. Smith of Multnomah County demanded that Lewis be located, and the Sergeant-At-Arms was sent off in search of him. He returned to report that Lewis had locked himself in a third floor committee room! After some delay, Lewis returned to the floor of the House, and debate on the bill resumed. Mrs. Thompson chided Lewis, reminding him that in 1917 he had introduced a far more radical bill which would have permitted intermarriage. Lewis claimed that he was forced to introduce that bill, but had supported it nevertheless. During the roll call vote, Lewis tried to escape again, but was brought back and cast a negative vote, claiming that the public accommodations bill was unconstitutional. In spite of the way the bill was treated, it received twenty-four favorable votes. Thirty-one negative votes defeated the bill.[31]

---

a While Rowan and Cannady were prominent members of Portland's African American community, Micco Harjo is more obscure. He was a mixed-race man of Black and either Muscogee (Creek) or Seminole heritage from Oklahoma, and a Spanish-American War veteran. He and his wife moved to Portland in 1913, where he was a member of the Black Elks Lodge and she in the Dahlia Temple. See Patricia Sanders' "Montavilla Memories" blog in *Village Portland*, December 2020.

A public accommodations bill was not introduced for another fourteen years.[32] In 1933 the NAACP persuaded five Senators from Multnomah County to introduce a bill in the Senate. The bill read,

> Any person who shall deny to any person because of race, creed or color the full enjoyment of any of the accommodations, advantages, facilities or privileges of any place of public resort, accommodation, assemblage or amusement, shall be deemed guilty of a misdemeanor and upon conviction thereof, shall be punished by a fine of not less than $25.00 nor more than $100.00, or by imprisonment in the county jail for not less than 90 days, or both such fine and imprisonment.[33]

The bill was passed to the Committee on Revision of Laws, where it was reported back to the Senate without recommendation. Only one of the Senators who had introduced the bill, Dorothy M. Lee, was willing to speak in favor of passage.[b] It came up for final vote and was defeated by a vote of nine in favor, nineteen opposed, and two absent.[34] The *Oregon Voter* commented on the bill's defeat:

> Race prejudice causes social discrimination against colored people and some whites. Resented, this discrimination creates a sense of inferiority which expresses itself in attempts to gain by law that which is unattainable by voluntary concession. S.B. 228 is a product of this inferiority complex. It is intended to force hotel proprietors, restaurants, auto camps, theaters and other service institutions to risk offense to the race prejudice of the great bulk of their patrons by admitting and seating members of races against whom these prejudices are felt. Obviously, legislation of this kind, if enforced, would merely accentuate and aggravate these prejudices, and bring into contempt the very people for whom it is sought to attain social equality.[35]

The article points out that any attempt to legislate racial toleration would send people into "hoodlum organizations" like the K.K.K., and said it would have been better if the bill had never been introduced.

> Want of tact and caution in approaching these huge problems is on the border line of irresponsibility.[36]

b That senator, Dorothy M. Lee, later became the first female mayor of Portland. As mayor, Lee led the push for a public accommodations bill for the city in 1951. It was advanced to the ballot, but the voters rejected the measure. See Meryl Lipman, "Dorothy McCullough Lee (1902–1981)," *Oregon Encyclopedia* (2021).

The *Advocate* also commented on the bill's defeat.

> From all appearances, it seems that after the member of the Multnomah County delegation introduced the bill, which by the way, is no feat at all they summarily forgot about it or had very little influence upon other members of the Senate. Enough members joined in introducing the bill so that when they returned home if anyone jumped on them about it they would have nearly all of Multnomah delegation to jump on and the old saying holds true, in numbers there is strength. At any rate those who voted for the bill kept their promise. And that's something, but we don't believe they went out of their way to get others to support the bill. The voters might look into this a little closer before next election.[37]

Similar bills were introduced into the Senate in 1937 and 1939, and from then on practically every legislative session considered a public accommodations bill until one was finally approved in 1953.

In 1937 a bill was sponsored jointly by three black organizations: The NAACP, Eugene Minor, President; Portland Negro Progressive League, Wyatt Williams, President; and Edgar Williams, a black delegate from the Labor Council. The bill was introduced, not because the black community was demanding complete social equality, but "only a right to live and earn an honest living."[38] The black delegation pointed out that this bill would not hurt the business of the more exclusive establishments because black people could not afford to patronize them. Black people, however, could never count on obtaining hotel accommodations, and this hurt the black businessman and tourist.

The bill was introduced in the Senate by Homer D. Angell, from Multnomah County, and was referred to the Judiciary Committee, where all but one member recommended that the bill be defeated. Their report was adopted, and the bill was permanently tabled.

In 1939, a similar bill, sponsored by the NAACP and the Oregon Commonwealth Federation, was introduced by a bipartisan group of five Senators and seven Representatives. All of the legislators who put their names on the bill were from Multnomah County, except for J. F. Hosh, an Independent from Deschutes County. It became Senate Bill 102, and was again referred to the Judiciary Committee. A hearing was held, and more than three hundred persons attended, including a large delegation of black people from Portland. Those who spoke in favor of the bill included Irvin M. Flowers, who testified that he had served in the armed forces in World War I, and when he returned to Portland was refused a dish of ice cream by a restaurant owner before he had taken off his uniform. Isadore Maney, a mail clerk for many years, said that he had recently been refused hotel accommodations in Bend. Mrs. John Lewis, representing the Portland YWCA, said that delegates to a National Negro Convention in Portland had been unable to find hotel accommodations and had to sleep in Pullman cars in the railroad yard. Others who spoke in favor of the bill were Edgar Williams, Nettie Rankin Ballard, who represented the Portland High School Teachers Association, and Irvin Goodman, a white Portland attorney.

The Oregon Hotel Association and the Oregon Apartment House Owners Association sent representatives to argue against the bill. They said that mixing whites and blacks as guests in the same hotel was bad for business, and cited cases where tenants had threatened to move from apartment houses when Chinese and black people moved in.

The Judiciary Committee sent the bill back to the floor of the Senate without recommendation. It was passed in the Senate, February 22, 1939. The vote was sixteen in favor, twelve opposed, two abstaining.[39] The bill then went to the House, where it was assigned to the Judiciary Committee. A vote to bring it to the full House failed. The *Oregon Voter* commented:

> Owners of hotels, eating establishments and places of recreation and amusement were in a dither, particularly after the Senate passed the bill. Should the measure become law they could see their businesses harmed by the patronage of the colored race. There was a fear that its provisions might serve to embolden colored folk to take advantage of the situation, or that the business concerns might become subject to payment of tribute to unscrupulous schemers, both white and black. The difficulty is not that many men themselves lack respect for the colored folk, but that they feel compelled for business reasons to cater to the small minority who do carry a prejudice. The hearings were interesting. Presentations by and on behalf of the colored folk were enlightening. The problems of these folk were explained so clearly as to elicit sincere sympathy for them. But in the final show-down the spirit of fellowship had to succumb before the cold unfeeling negation of mercenary considerations and the bill died in the hand s of the house Judiciary committee. Efforts to bring the bill out of the hands of the committee failed.[40]

A public accommodations bill was finally passed in 1953, and further revised in 1973. The combined vote in 1953 was 67 in favor, 20 opposed. The text of the law as it now stands is contained in the Oregon Revised Statutes, 30.670.[41]

The westward migration of American black people began in the first fifty years of the nineteenth century. Many black people saw the West as an unsettled region where greater economic and political freedom was possible. The free states and territories in the West presented an opportunity for some to escape slavery. What these black people found when they came to the Pacific Coast states of Oregon, Washington, and California were many of the same conditions and attitudes they had hoped to escape. In many ways, Oregon had the least to offer. Although the differences in the legislative record in these three states does not necessarily signify a difference in attitudes toward racial minorities, basic civil rights legislation did provide the legal clout black people needed in order to begin to attain better jobs, fair housing, and equal enjoyment of public accommodations. A comparison of the legislative record of California, Washington, and Oregon provides a significant index of the degree to which black people were able to advance their economic and social conditions, and to a lesser extent the degree of racial prejudice they had to face.

The first non-Indian occupation of California began as a result of Spanish exploration and conquest, and among those who settled in California were blacks, Zambos (half black, half Indian), and Afro-Spaniards, descendants of slaves brought to the New World to work plantations in Mexico. Many intermarried with the local population, and by 1794 nearly one-quarter of California's population was classified as mulatto.[c] The Mexican officials did not discriminate against the black population: Manuel Victoria, Jose Figueroa, and Pico Pico, three Spanish governors of California, had some African ancestry.[42]

With the arrival of large numbers of Americans, many coming to work in the mining regions, anti-black sentiment began to surface. Settlers brought slaves to work the mines, and free black people were numerous in the mining regions. The resultant mix of free blacks, slaves, and whites was viewed with great resentment by non-slaveholding whites. In some cases, white people refused to work in areas where black people were working, claiming that it was demeaning to work side by side with them. In one case, white miners succeeded in driving out several Texas slave owners and their slaves. Free black people faced restrictions similar to those found in the East. Often they were segregated into separate rooming houses, hotels and restaurants,

c The author cites a work by Dr. Quintard Taylor for this claim; however, Dr. Taylor gives a different figure in his 1998 book *In Search of a Racial Frontier: African Americans in the American West 1528–1990* (New York: W. W. Norton & Co., 1998): "Approximately 55 percent of the Spanish speaking population in California was of mixed heritage, according to historian Jack Forbes, and 20 percent possessed some African ancestry."

particularly in the larger mining towns and in San Francisco.

Racial issues were raised at numerous meetings held to discuss the creation of a state government, and the majority opinion was anti-slavery and anti-black. When California's constitution was formulated in a state convention in 1849, national anti-slavery and anti-black sentiment had not reached the fever pitch of the mid 1850s, and despite strong support for an exclusion clause the majority felt that racist statements might jeopardize California's admission to the Union. An exclusion clause was rejected. The constitution did bar blacks and Indians from voting, and banned slavery. The voters of California approved the constitution and elected as state governor Peter Burnett. He had lived in Oregon for several years prior to moving to California, and continued to press for anti-black legislation in California. He failed to gain majority support for another exclusion law, but two other anti-black bills were passed in 1850. Anyone having 1/6th Negro blood was defined as black, and barred from testifying in court against a white person. Intermarriage was also banned.

The 1852 legislature, prompted by an increase in the black population from 700 to 2,200, considered two measures to discourage further immigration of blacks, or reduce the number of black people already there. Another exclusion law was introduced and defeated, but a fugitive slave law was approved, which allowed slaveowners to reclaim black people who had been their slaves prior to California's admission to the Union. This law was allowed to lapse in 1855, but was invoked by Burnett in his ruling in the State Supreme Court in the case of the ex-slave, Archy Lee.

In 1858 the exclusion of black people was still being proposed.[43] The exclusion law introduced that year would have required black people to register and carry papers proving that their residence in California was legal. This bill passed in the House but was defeated in the Senate, but not before the proposal so enraged black residents that 100 of them left California to settle in British Columbia.

As early as 1852, black people organized to repeal the law that prevented them from testifying in court. The first statewide Colored Convention met in 1855, and lobbied against this law and segregation in the public schools. They continued to lobby and petition the state legislature until the anti-testimony law was repealed in 1863.

School district funds were first based on the number of white children only, and black people had to organize private schools. In 1866 school appropriations were still based on the number of white children only, but in that year black people were given the first legal recognition of their right to public education. After 1875 the dual school system gradually began to disappear. Some legislative gains were realized between 1863 and 1875, but not enough to initiate a period of racial justice and tolerance.

California, like Oregon, ratified the Thirteenth and Fourteenth Amendments, but again, like Oregon, did not ratify the Fifteenth Amendment until the mid-twentieth century. The prohibition on interracial marriages was ruled unconstitutional in 1948. A civil rights act, based on the federal laws of 1875, was passed in 1897, and a public accommodations law was passed in 1905. The first black state legislator was elected in 1919, and employment opportunities for black people in education and other professional fields began to open up.

Washington did not become a state until 1889, and was not directly involved in the anti-black and anti-slavery controversy preceding the Civil War. In 1855 the territorial legislature petitioned Congress to secure the donation land claim of George Bush. In 1887 the legislature repealed the law banning intermarriage. The original state constitution contained a clause banning racial discrimination in education. In 1890 Washington adopted a civil rights law based on the federal laws of 1875, and in 1909 passed a public accommodations law.

Both California and Washington passed legislation in the twentieth century preventing members of the Ku Klux Klan from wearing hoods to conceal their identity. Oregon had no such law. Black state representatives were elected in California and Washington much earlier than in Oregon. Clearly, Oregon lagged behind its Pacific Coast neighbors in civil rights legislation before 1940. Yet all three states had large Oriental populations which received much of the brunt of racial antagonisms, and all three areas were settled by white Americans who brought their anti-slavery, anti-black racial baggage with them.

The natural resources of both California and Washington are superior to those of Oregon, which contributed to a larger population, more wealth, and the development of an urban and cosmopolitan society. Trends toward urbanization in both states are more widespread, while Oregon is still largely rural.

Oregon, progressive in many ways, resisted the necessary legislation which would correct historical inequalities in the treatment of blacks and other minorities. In the absence of a significant black population before 1940 that could effect legislation, it remained a West Coast ecological paradise with a peculiar resistance to change.

10

A Tough Spot with a Nice Climate

Epilogue

In the decade of the 1940s two unlikely events, a World War and a flood, became the catalysts for a minor revolution that was to usher in a new age for Portland's black community. In 1942 Americans were gearing up for war production, and Portland became a shipbuilding center. The shortage of available labor was so acute that the Kaiser Company recruited workers from the East and South, bringing them to Oregon on trains dubbed "Magic Carpet Specials." Many black people were recruited and came, attracted by the promise of good jobs and high wages. Estimates vary, but between 20,000 and 25,000 black people came to Portland in the early 1940s; white migration into Portland was about 100,000.

Portland was unprepared for a mass influx of people, and more particularly for the numbers of black people who came. Overnight the black community was transformed from a nearly invisible minority to a large, visible one. In typical fashion, the white community resisted change. There was evidence of a racist backlash; the war period saw a distinct proliferation of Jim Crow signs in restaurants and saloons. Mayor Earl Riley was quoted as saying, "Portland can absorb only a minimum of Negroes without upsetting the city's regular life."[1]

The new black people were initially viewed with alarm by members of the settled black community. In many cases the two groups had little in common other than their racial identity. Blacks were fearful that the small gains they had made would be wiped out and that Oregonians would react by initiating more restrictive legislation. The new blacks represented a wider cross-section than was previously evident in Portland: there were a number of well educated blacks from the Midwest and East, as well as rural southern blacks who were unaccustomed to city ways and had never voted. There was also the inevitable fringe group of characters who came to Oregon for the ride and never picked up a blow torch or welding iron, prompting Bill Berry, Executive Secretary of the Urban League, to say,

> The only Negroes the Urban League wants to help are the decent, hard-working and self-respecting colored people who want to earn their rightful places as good citizens in every meaning of the word.[2]

Despite any mixed feelings the black community may have had, they quickly recognized that an increase in the black population represented a potential enhancement of their political clout. Both the NAACP and the newly formed Urban League became involved in voter education and registration programs in the housing projects at Guilds Lake and Vanport.

Initially, job opportunities were a disappointment to the black workers. When they applied for jobs in the shipyards, they were told that nothing was available, and many help wanted notices specified "white only." Although the Kaiser Company had promised good jobs, local unions resisted integration, a prerequisite for skilled jobs under the closed shop system. One union leader, Tom Ray, boss of Local 72 of the Boilermaker's Union, said he would "pull the place down" rather than give black people equal job rights at the Kaiser Portland yards.[3]

After pressure from the NAACP, the Kaiser Brothers, a federal inspection team, and a reprimand from President Roosevelt, the unions compromised and more skilled jobs were opened to black workers, but only for the duration of the war. Blacks were allowed to work in union controlled shops and paid union dues, but were denied the benefits of union membership. The Boilermakers and Shipbuilders Union, which had control of 65 percent of the A.F. of L. shipyard workers, set up separate black auxiliary unions. Frequently, local union attitudes determined racist policies. The Longshoreman's Union, which had a national policy of non-discrimination, referred blacks to jobs in Portland only to have white union members refuse to work with them. After threats to call a general work stoppage, the black workers were removed from the job. A similar situation occurred in the A.F. of L. Laundry Worker's Union in Portland.[4]

Black workers were able to earn good money during the war, but once the war was over they had no job security or seniority, and most were fired. In 1947, three months after one-third of the city's twelve thousand black workers lost their jobs, Julius A. Thomas, Industrial Relations Director for the National Urban League, came to Portland, voicing the frustrations of the black community and classifying Portland as "just like any southern town . . . the most prejudiced [city] in the west."[5]

After the war the black community, courtesy of war time economics and union policies, had new problems to deal with. Unemployment became a major concern, and those who could not find work had to subsist on welfare and unemployment payments. The Urban League took an active role in finding jobs for black people, negotiating with employers and sending out hand-picked qualified workers to jobs previously held only by whites.

Another problem for both the settled black community and the war workers was the shortage of decent housing: predictions made by the *Advocate* in 1930 were becoming a reality.[6] The Albina area, historically a white working class neighborhood, was gradually being transformed into a black ghetto. Before the war, black people had moved into Albina and northeast Portland for various reasons: the proximity of the railroad yards, a general shift of population to the east side, and the proximity of black churches and social institutions. In the 1930s definitions of non-segregated areas began to emerge: the rule of thumb followed by the real estate industry was that if there was a black-occupied residence within four blocks, the area could not be defined as a white segregated neighborhood.[7] The policies of the real estate establishment and the indifference of the city housing authority fostered the patterns of segregated housing which emerged during and after the war.

During the war, housing was scarce for both black and white workers. A few temporary facilities and the company-built dormitories were inadequate; some black men were forced to sleep on billiard tables in taverns, or in churches. They were excluded from the city-wide housing market, and confined to the housing that was available in the Williams Avenue area and a dormitory in Vancouver. White citizens of the Albina area opposed construction of a dormitory on NE Flint Street intended to house black workers, claiming that the black population on the east side had increased from two thousand to more than five thousand, and that more crimes had been committed in the area than in the previous thirty years. Dr. Vern Wirtz, President of the Central East Portland Community Club was quoted as saying,

> If it is necessary to bring in large numbers of Negro workers, locate them on the edge of the city . . . It would be much better for all concerned. If they are allowed to fan out through the city, it will be necessary to station a policeman on every block to prevent what some Negroes are pulling around here.[8]

William Greene, President of the Colored Republican Club, countered charges that attributed the increase in crime to black people.

> We want to convey to the citizens of Portland that the influx of labor is bringing in undesirables of all races . . . The Negro population of Portland should not be criticized for what one or two Negroes do.[9]

Other churches and social groups supported the position of Greene and other black people, and requested that the Portland Council of Churches petition the federal housing authority to provide adequate housing for the black defense workers. The Reverend J. J. Clow, pastor of the Mount Olivet Baptist Church, pleaded for an open housing policy in the city. He warned that tensions in Albina between blacks and whites were approaching a dangerous level, and might result in serious consequences if not relieved. He claimed that anti-black sentiment was the result of "police hysteria" and "damaging newspaper publicity," and said that the police were arresting innocent people. Among white church leaders some reservations were expressed. The Reverend Charles Elrey, a retired Presbyterian minister, said that trouble resulted in cities where integrated housing was tried. He felt that black people would be "better off . . . if restricted to certain districts."[10] Mayor Earl Riley felt that the situation was bad, but could be handled. Admitting that the city could only absorb a minimum of black people, he pointed out that in war-time conditions the community must "forget some of [its] previous ideals."[11]

Housing projects for defense workers were developed in the Vanport and Guilds Lake areas. By 1945, 5,808 black people found housing in Vancouver, Washington. Within the housing projects spot segregation was practiced. After the war, whites and some blacks hoped the black workers would go back where they came from, and many did. But many also stayed, and had the usual trouble finding adequate housing within the metropolitan area. The *Oregonian* published a report in 1945 speculating on the post war outlook for blacks in Portland, quoting Mayor Riley, who again denied that a race problem existed. The article stated that integrated housing had been a success in Vancouver, with only a minimum of racial friction. Black leaders feared that with the end of the war, the remaining black people would be forced to live in temporary housing projects, or in restricted areas in Portland. The housing available for sale to black people in Albina was in areas steadily converting to business and commercial interests, making land values high and houses substandard. They were residential districts bound to deteriorate further, and poor investments. The housing shortage was universal and, as usual, the needs of black people were the last to be considered. The "do-nothing" policy of the housing officials, black people feared, would make Portland another "tough spot with a nice climate."[12]

In 1947 the Urban League of Portland took the Housing Authority to task for not enforcing the official federal policy of non-discrimination in housing. The Housing Authority's local policy was to separate tenants according to race, making it impossible to serve people on a first come, first served basis, a policy unfair to both blacks and whites. Some vacant housing in Vanport and Guilds Lake were unavailable to white people, because they were in an area designated for blacks only. The Urban League urged the Housing Authority to modify its policies, but little change resulted.

At the time of the Vanport flood, there were about 18,500 people, including 5,000 blacks, living in the housing project. It had not been intended as permanent housing, and would have been closed had other housing been available. The flood occurred May 30, 1948, and turned Vanport into a lake. All available housing was pressed into service, and many of the black people who were left homeless were taken in by families in the metropolitan area. While many of the stranded white families were able to leave town, black families, many subsisting on welfare and unemployment, did not have the financial resources to settle elsewhere. The resettlement of the flood victims, in the absence of any direct action taken by the city housing authorities, reinforced the patterns of segregation. One black resident recalled,

> We in the NAACP used to chide [Mayor Baker] about the segregated housing in Vanport. "Get the people in town!" "Where are you going to put them . . . there's no place for them . . ." Well, bless my soul, May 30, when that dike broke, they found a place for them. And what did they do? They congregated right down on Albina, in that area.[13]

The Portland Housing Authority did not integrate its operations until 1950, and even in 1957 was not offering housing to many black people. In that year it administered 433 temporary dwelling units, 137 of which were occupied by black families. Of 485 permanent housing units in the Columbia Villa and Dekum Court developments, only 30 units were occupied by black people. Meanwhile, living conditions in Albina were more crowded in 1957 than they had been in 1945, and the Portland Housing Authority was criticized for its indifference to the housing needs of Portland's black community. Beyond that, a Portland City Club study concluded:

> . . . most white Portlanders are unaware of the social and economic problems which face the city's Negro population. Responsible public

> officials have made little effort to publicize the presence of segregated housing and general slum conditions which we have found *do* exist.[14]

In the meantime, the Urban League addressed the problem of segregation as determined by the real estate industry. The official doctrine in the Realty Board's Code of Ethics that held that blacks depress property values had been abandoned in 1952. The practice of real estate agents remained virtually unchanged, despite claims to the contrary, such as one made in 1954 by an official of the Portland Realty Board:

> Realty boards do not under any circumstances have anything to do with segregation . . . We have only one thing in our code of ethics and that is never to sell property so that it will reduce the value of other properties in the area, and there can be a variety of reasons. It is the residents of the neighborhood who make the ruling.[15]

An Urban League study found that, contrary to widespread belief, property values were not depressed when blacks moved into a neighborhood. The findings were based on a study of five residential neighborhoods into which black people had moved and five areas that remained all white. No significant variation in the upward price trend of houses in the two groups was found.[16] The study also explored attitudes toward integrated housing, and found that those people who had had the most exposure to minority groups were more in favor of integrated housing than those who had no personal contact with minorities in their neighborhoods. Those favoring integration also tended to be younger and the parents of school age children. Those polled were almost equally divided between those who favored integrated housing and those who favored segregated housing. On the basis of expressed prejudice, the study found that 35 percent of those polled expressed little or no prejudice, 32 percent expressed moderate prejudice, and 33 percent expressed extreme prejudice.

In 1961 the League of Women Voters of Portland published a study that focused on awareness of the Oregon Fair Housing Law among both blacks and whites and sampled attitudes toward integrated housing. The study concluded that many whites were still convinced that when blacks moved into white neighborhoods property values suffered, and while some black people were able to move out of the Albina area, many were still having difficulties moving into other neighborhoods.

In 1976 seven elementary schools had minority enrollments of over 50 percent, and school segregation, reflecting over thirty years of segregated housing practices, is an issue which is still being resolved.[17]

Progress in other areas since the 1940s has been more encouraging. The state legislature, after defeating a fair employment practices act in 1947, passed a similar law two years later. In 1950 the city of Portland passed a comprehensive civil rights ordinance, but it was defeated in a general election. In 1951 discrimination in vocational schools was banned, and in 1953 a state public accommodations law was passed. In 1957 a Portland City Club Report noted that the public accommodations law had been "noticeably effective" in eliminating discrimination, but concluded:

> . . . widespread discrimination is still being practiced and will so long as the injured party must file suit.[18]

This report concluded that the greatest improvement for black people had been economic. Blacks had been able to get union jobs in the building trades, the dry cleaning industry, the foundries, and the construction and building service industries. A few unions still practiced discrimination, particularly evident in the reluctance of apprenticeship programs to admit black people.

Many blacks were finding jobs in the professions, in education, the federal civil service, state and county social work, medicine and nursing, the ministry, and the law. The professions of education and social work attracted the largest percent of black college graduates in Portland.

Public agencies also employed a number of black people. The city of Portland had 115 black employees, primarily in manual labor. The Police department had eight black employees, and the Fire department one. Multnomah County employed fifty blacks, and the State of Oregon forty, including an assistant state attorney general. The federal government had 275 black employees in Portland, and forty-six black teachers were employed by the Portland School district.

The principal area of weakness was in the business community, as employers were still reluctant to hire black people. The City Club report noted:

> . . . too often the lack of any policy is simply the reflection of a company's lack of any real interest in equal opportunities for Negroes, regardless of ability or training.[19]

The study concluded:

> We have discovered that some definite progress has been made, as it has throughout the country. But we have also found that prejudice and

> discrimination still exist in Portland, to the degree at least that most Negroes have not in any realistic sense been "harmoniously integrated" into Portland's community life.[20]

In 1972 the median family income of non-whites was $7,106, compared to white median family income of $11,549. The unemployment rate in the city of Portland in 1975 was 10.1 percent for whites, and 15.6 percent for blacks. Some believe that the gap has widened. A recent study concluded,

> Until the society decides to do something, the poor will continue to be poorer while the rich get richer.[21]

Portland's black community was profoundly and permanently altered. The war brought new problems and the beginning of solutions to old problems. For the first time, black people became the largest and most visible minority in Oregon. Black civil rights organizations were strengthened and new ones formed. New visibility resulted in the passage of basic civil rights legislation. Although these laws have had varying degrees of success in eliminating discrimination, they were preferable to no laws at all.

The war brought negative changes as well. There was an increase in racial tension, and hostility between "new" and "old" blacks. The power structure in the black community changed, and some former leaders, accustomed to dealing with the white power structure as members of a tiny minority, were labeled "Uncle Toms." War economics and union policies combined to foster the creation of a class of black people who subsisted by marginal and sometimes illegal methods. An equitable solution to integrated schools has yet to be found.

Despite a history of inequality, life for black people in Oregon was not devoid of joy or hope. One black Portlander recalled,

> I've had a grand life here in Portland. It's a good place to live. What I've always liked about it is that you could live like you wanted to. You could keep up with the crowd if you wanted or you could just live to yourself . . . I love my church and I loved the Federated Clubs when I was in them . . . I'm glad to see there are some good people here. Some good people have come in here and have helped to make [Portland] continue [to be a] good place to live . . . I just felt Portland was growing up when a lot of things happened.[22]

In many ways the black people of Oregon are our community's twentieth century pioneers. Like pioneers of any age, they are accustomed to survival. Many of the values that our society has forgotten are retained in the black community: the value of education, strong family and religious ties, a sense of tradition and respect for our elder citizens, a sensitivity to the needs of the less fortunate. We ignore these deep and pervasive values at the peril of our collective human spirit.

Afterword

My whole-hearted gratitude to those who made the re-publication of this book possible: to Irene Zenev and the Benton County Historical Society for acquiring the copyright and passing it along to Oregon Black Pioneers, and to Zachary Stocks of OBP, for his work in updating the notes and photographs. OBP, a non-profit organization, will receive all royalties from sales of this book. Finally, to OSU Press and director Thomas Booth for ushering this new edition into the world.

The past forty-two years has been a journey for all of us; for me, particularly since the election of 2016, one that involved a long look into the mirror of American history and the twin tragedies of genocide and slavery, which, like a wound that has never healed, continue to fester and poison us all. Fortunately, I have found good companions in the flowering of diverse voices in poetry, fiction, and nonfiction, and of the many, many books I have read, I would like to mention three that offer connections to the larger world and speak to the need to bring this iteration of Oregon's black history back into the world.

I want to thank Michelle Lewis, the owner, with her husband, Charles Hannah, of Third Eye Books in Portland, a 100 percent black-owned and operated business. She handed me a copy of *Post Traumatic Slave Syndrome: America's Legacy of Enduring Injury and Healing*. Dr. Joy DeGruy, a professional in the mental health field and former professor at Portland State University, encourages people to view their lives through the lens of history and thereby build resilience. Access to history, including local history, is therefore essential to the healing process.

A second book is Isabel Wilkerson's epic history, *The Warmth of Other Suns*. Among the many threads of this American journey is the story of Dr. Robert P. Foster, who left Monroe, Louisiana, and settled in California. Like other immigrants who may have had professional credentials in their home country but had to take jobs as laborers or taxi drivers, Foster's mortician friend worked as a laborer in Oakland. Foster's mentor, Dr. William Beck, established a practice in Los Angeles but he and his wife had to fight restrictive covenants to buy a nice home in a white neighborhood. Moving in, they were greeted by a burning cross on their front lawn. Foster himself eventually established a successful medical practice, yet was still vulnerable to the unwritten codes of northern racism, and near the end of his life was humiliated by an unfair professional demotion. As Wilkerson narrates, "He had made it to the paradise he had so believed in all those decades ago that he had bragged about it before even seeing it. Now, it had betrayed him in ways he could not have imagined" (p. 462). Although Wilkerson does not include Oregon in her discussion, readers familiar with immigration will find many parallels. Wilkerson's discussion of the loss of southern family, culture, and familiar place applies as well to the many immigrants who sought a new life in Oregon.

My third prized possession is Mitchell S. Jackson's *Survival Math: Notes on an All-American Family*. He chooses to begin his searing memoir with a hypothetical letter to Markus Lopez, the first black person of record to die in what would become Oregon. The young sailor, who had barely stepped foot on land, was killed by native people in a dispute over a cutlass. From Lopez's death on August 16, 1788, to Jackson's own birth in Portland on August 16, 1975, he recounts in his lively, street-wise prose the historic struggles and accomplishments of his forebears, reaching back into the past to contextualize his own and his generation's struggle to survive and thrive in a place that, as he concludes, "ain't our Eden, and won't be, for that was never their intent" (p. 12).

It's not rocket science to admit that Oregon is still "a tough place with a nice climate," but it is my fervent hope that this new edition, which will now be widely available to an audience young and old, can once again be in conversation with the newer generations of books and writers. Acknowledging the truth of our collective past is the first necessary step forward into a more hopeful, healing, and resilient future together.

Elizabeth McLagan
March 2022

Acknowledgments

Oregon Black History Project Task Group

Elizabeth Buehler
Field Historical, Editor
Oregon Historical Society

Verne Duncan
Superintendent of Public Instruction
Representatives:
Jerry Fuller*
Director of Compensatory Education

Herman Washington*
Specialist, Social Studies

William Greaby
Vice President, Regional Loan Supervisor
U.S. National Bank

Ernest Hartzog
Assistant Superintendent for Staff Development and Community Relations
Portland Public Schools
the Reverend L. Fisher Hines, Task Group Chairman
Bethel A.M.E. Church

E. Kimbark MacColl*
Historian, Writer, Adjunct Professor of History
Portland State University

Barbara Miller*
Director of Development
University of Portland

Darrell Millner*
Associate Professor of Black Studies
Portland State University

Bobbie Nunn*
Desegregation Specialist
Portland Public Schools

Warne Nunn
Assistant: Vice President and Manager, Portland District
Pacific Power and Light

Warren Robinson, Sr.
Multnomah Kennel Club, Public Relations

Otto Rutherford*
Retired Director, Urban League Senior Service Center
Past President, NAACP

Thomas Sloan
Manager of Employee Relations
Tektronix, Inc.

Marie Smith*
Recipient, Russell Peyton Award, 1978
Past President NAACP, Oregon Association of Colored
Women's Clubs, Board Member, YMCA

Helen Warbington
Assistant: Director, Case Management Unit
Human Resources Bureau
*denotes member of Editorial Committee

Former members of the Task Group include Robert Blanchard, Keith Burns, Geri Christian, Gloria Fisher, Cleveland Gilcrease, Gary Gomez, Ruth Haefner, William Harris, Hazel Hays, A. Lee Henderson, Erma Hepburn, Herman Huston, Leland Johnson, Henry Scott, Herb Simpson, and Lizzie Weeks.

Other individuals who have aided the project include Richard D. Bach, Rives, Bonyhacli, Drummond & Smith; Sam Blanchard; Anita Book, Klamath County Museum; John C. Broderick, Library of Congress; Genevive S. Burk, M.D.; Ivan Cannady; David Duniway, Mission Mill Museum; Mrs. Millard Elkins; Richard H. Engman, Jacksonville Museum; Wilmer Gardner, Clackamas County Historical Society; Lesta Gamer; Mr. and Mrs. Vernon Gaskins; Green Thumb Garden Center; Irene Helms, Crook County Historical Society; Kenneth Holmes; Gwendolyn Hooker; Janice J. Justice, Herman and Eliza Oliver Historical Museum; Paul Keady; Mary Ringo King; Virginia Leach; Laura Legler; Mr. and Mrs. Bill McClenndon; Robert Marsh, Polk County Museum; Lloyd Meyer, Washington County Museum; Mrs. Arthur Nelson; Evelyn Parry; Mrs. Phil Reynolds; Leslie Shaw; Lucy Skjelstad, Horner Museum; Dorothy Stofiel, Columbia County Historical Society; Patricia Stone, Lincoln County Historical Society; Mr. and Mrs. James Sullivan; Betty Thompson; T.F. Tomlin; and Dorothy Weiss.

Manuscripts and Published Materials

The author wishes to acknowledge permission to publish materials from the manuscript collections of the Oregon Historical Society, The Oregon Black History Project, the Jacksonville Museum, the Oregon State Archives, and from the Special Collections Library of the University of Oregon. She also acknowledges permission to reprint from the following published works:

Blacks in Oregon, a Statistical and Historical Report, by Little & Weiss, ed. ©1978, Portland State University.

"Report on the Negro in Portland: A Progress Report 1945-1957." ©1966, City Club of Portland.

The Growth of a City. Power and Politics in Portland, Oregon 1915-1950, by E. Kimbark MacColl, ©1979, E. Kimbark MacColl.

The Shaping of a City. Business and Politics in Portland, Oregon 1885-1915, by E. Kimbark MacColl, ©1976, E. Kimbark MacColl.

"Black Harris, Mountain Man, Teller of Tales," by Verne Bright, *Oregon Historical Quarterly*, Vol. 52 (March 1951), ©1951 by the Oregon Historical Society.

"Recollections of an Old Pioneer, " by Peter H. Burnett, *Oregon Historical Quarterly*, Vol. 5 (March 1904), ©1904 by the Oregon Historical Society.

'The Slavery Question in Oregon," by T. W. Davenport, *Oregon Historical Quarterly*, Vol. 9 (Sept. 1908), ©1908 by the Oregon Historical Society.

"Dr. Robert Newell, Pioneer," by T. C. Elliot, *Oregon Historical Quarterly*, Vol. 9 (June 1908), ©1908 by the Oregon Historical Society.

"Reminiscences," by John Minto, *Oregon Historical Quarterly*, Vol. 2 (Sept. 1901), ©1901 by the Oregon Historical Society.

"22 Letters of David Logan, Pioneer Oregon Lawyer, " by Henry Platt, ed., *Oregon Historical Quarterly*, Vol. 44 (Sept. 1943), ©1943 by the Oregon Historical Society.

"James Douglas on the Columbia, 1830-1849, " by W. Sage, *Oregon Historical Quarterly*, Vol. 27 (Dec. 1926), ©1926 by the Oregon Historical Society.

"Political History of Oregon," by George H. Williams, *Oregon Historical Quarterly*, Vol. 2 (March 1901), ©1901 by the Oregon Historical Society.

"Political Parties in Oregon," by W.C. Woodward, *Oregon Historical Quarterly*, Vol. 12 (June 1911), ©1911 by the Oregon Historical Society.

Appendix

Oregon Population Statistics

Year	Total Population	Black Population	Black Population as % Total
1850	13,294	54	0.41
1860	52,465	128	0.24
1870	90,922	346	0.38
1880	174,768	487	0.28
1890	317,704	1,186	0.37
1900	413,536	1,105	0.27
1910	672,765	1,492	0.22
1920	783,389	2,144	0.27
1930	953,786	2,234	0.23
1940	1,089,684	2,565	0.24
1950	1,521,341	11,529	0.76
1960	1,768,687	18,133	1.03
1970	2,091,533	26,308	1.26

Oregon Exclusion Act (June 1844) and Amended Act (December 1844)

AN ACT in regard to Slavery and Free Negroes and Mulattoes.
Be it enacted by the Legislative Committee of Oregon as follows:

SECTION 1. That slavery and involuntary servitude shall be for ever prohibited in Oregon.

SEC. 2. That in all cases where slaves shall have been, or shall hereafter be, brought into Oregon, the owners of such slaves respectively shall have the term of three years from the introduction of such slaves to remove them out of the country.

SEC. 3. That if such owners of slaves shall neglect or refuse to remove such slaves from the country within the time specified in the preceding section, such slaves shall be free.

SEC. 4. That when any free negro or mulatto shall have come to Oregon, he or she (as the case may be), if of the age of eighteen or upward, shall remove from and leave the country within the term of two years for males and three years for females from the passage of this act; and that if any free negro or mulatto shall hereafter come to Oregon, if of the age aforesaid, he or she shall quit and leave the country within the term of two years for males and three years for females from his or her arrival in the country.

SEC. 5. That if such free negro or mulatto be under the age aforesaid, the terms of time specified in the preceding section shall begin to run when he or she shall arrive at such age.

SEC. 6. That if any such free negro or mulatto shall fail to quit the country as required by this act, he or she may be arrested upon a warrant issued by some justice of the peace, and, if guilty upon trial before such justice, shall receive upon his or her bare back not less than twenty nor more than thirty-nine stripes, to be inflicted by the constable of the proper county.

SEC. 7. That if any free negro or mulatto shall fail to quit the country within the term of six months after receiving such stripes, he or she shall again receive the same punishment once in every six months until he or she shall quit the country.

SEC. 8. That when any slave shall obtain his or her freedom, the time specified in the fourth section shall begin to run from the time when such freedom shall be obtained.

Passed by the Legislative Committee of the provisional government of Oregon, June 26, 1844.

AN ACT amendatory of an Act passed June 26, 1844, in regard to slavery and for other purposes.

Be it enacted by the Legislative Committee of Oregon as follows:

SECTION 1. That the sixth and seventh sections of said act are hereby repealed.

SEC. 2. That if any such free negro or mulatto shall fail to quit and leave the country, as required by the act to which this is amendatory, he or she may be arrested upon a warrant issued by some justice of the peace; and if guilty upon trial before such justice had, the said justice shall issue his order to any officer competent to execute process, directing said officer to give ten days' public notice, by at least four written or printed advertisements, that he will publicly hire out such free negro or mulatto to the lowest bidder, on a day and at a place therein specified. On the day and at the place mentioned in said notice, such officer shall expose such free negro or mulatto to public hiring; and the person who will obligate himself to remove such free negro or mulatto from the country for the shortest term of service, shall enter into a bond with good and sufficient security to Oregon, in a penalty of at least one thousand dollars, binding himself to remove said negro or mulatto out of the country within six months after such service shall expire; which bond shall be filed in the clerk's office in the proper county; and upon failure to perform the conditions of said bond, the attorney prosecuting for Oregon shall commence a suit upon a certified copy of such bond in the circuit court against such delinquent and his sureties.

Passed by the Legislative Committee, December 19, 1844.

The Constitution of the State of Oregon: Pertinent Sections (drafted 1857, ratified 1859)

Article 1 (Section 31). – White foreigners who are, or may hereafter become residents of this State shall enjoy the same rights in respect to the possession, enjoyment, and descent of property as native born citizens. And the Legislative Assembly shall have power to restrain, and regulate the immigration to this State of persons not qualified to become Citizens of the United States.

Article 1 (Section 34). – There shall be neither slavery, nor involuntary servitude in the State, otherwise than as a punishment for crime, whereof the party shall have been duly convicted.

Article 1 (Section 35). – No free negro, or mulatto, not residing in this State at the time of the adoption of this Constitution, shall come, reside, or be within this State, or hold any real estate, or make any contracts, or maintain any suit therein; and the Legislative Assembly shall provide by penal laws, for the removal, by public officers, of all such negroes, and mulattoes, and for their effectual exclusion from the State, and for the punishment of persons who shall bring them into the state, or employ, or harbor them. (repealed November 3, 1926)

Article II (Section 6). – No Negro, Chinaman, or Mulatto shall have the right of suffrage. (repealed June 28, 1927)

Article XV (Section 8). – No Chinaman, not a resident of the State at the adoption of this Constitution, shall ever hold any real estate, or mining claim, or work any mining claim therein. The Legislative Assembly shall provide by law in the most effectual manner for carrying out the above provisions.

Oregon Public Accommodations Law (1953)

Oregon Revised Statutes
30.670 Right of all persons to equal facilities in places of public accommodations. All persons within the jurisdiction of this state shall be entitled to the full and equal accommodations, advantages, facilities and privileges of any place of public accommodation, without any distinction, discrimination or restriction on account of race, religion, sex, marital status, color or national origin.

Notes

Chapter 1

1 Howay, *Voyages of the "Columbia" to the Northwest Coast*, p. 6.
2 Ibid., 32–33.
3 Bancroft, *History of the Northwest Coast*, Vol. 1, p. 706.
4 Bancroft, *History of the Northwest Coast*, Vol. 1, p. 708.
5 Thwaites, *Original Journals of Lewis and Clark*, Vol. 5, p. 290.
6 Thwaites, *Original Journals of Lewis and Clark*, Vol. 5, p. 358.
7 Hosmer, *Gass's Journal of the Lewis and Clark Expedition*, p.xxxiv.
8 Bakeless, *Lewis and Clark: Partners in Discovery*, p. 443. The identity of the black chief living among the Crow Indians is disputed. It has also been ascribed to Jim Beckwourth and Edward Rose. Bancroft, op. cit., Vol. 2, p. 85.
9 Rucker, *The Oregon Trail and Some of Its Blazers*, p. 146–7.
10 Irving, *Astoria, or Anecdotes of an Enterprise Beyond the Rocky Mountains*, footnote, p. 223.
11 Henderson, "Introduction of the Negroes Into the Pacific Northwest 788–1842," pp. 34–36.
12 Drury, *Marcus and Narcissa Whitman and the Opening of Old Oregon*, p. 231.
13 Lee, *Ten Years in Oregon*, pp. 224–5.
14 See Chapter 2.
15 *Oregon Spectator*, September 2, 1851.
16 Ibid., December 24, 1846.
17 *Oregon Spectator*, August 6, 1846. An account of his life published in the *Oregon Native Son* mentions that he attempted to pilot the Schooner Shad across the Columbia River bar. The account published in the *Oregon Spectator* in 1846 mentions a similar incident, without naming the pilot. "After passing Baker's Bay, the Shark was run upon Chinook Shoal, through the unskillfulness of a negro man found living at the Cape, who undertook to pilot her over to Astoria. She was however gotten off in a few hours, having suffered no perceptible damage." The Columbia Bar has been historically a treacherous crossing. Appendix and Notes/189
18 McDonald, Lucile, "Cape Disappointment's First Settler," *Seattle Times*, November 22, 1964.
19 *Oregon Spectator*, December 30, 1851.
20 Holmes, "James Douglas," pp. 140–1, and Kilian, *Go Do Some Great Thing*, p. 30.
21 Sage, "James Douglas on the Columbia, 1830–1849," p. 367.
22 McLaughlin's Fort Vancouver Letters, first series, James Douglas to the Governor and Committee, March 16, 1831, p. 242, quoted in Winther, The Old Oregon Country, p. 104.
23 Burnett, "Recollections of An Old Pioneer," p. 94.
24 Thorton, *Oregon and California in 1848*, pp. 14–15.
25 Peltier, "Moses, 'Black' Harris," p. 103.

26 Ibid., p. 109, quoted from Ross, Marvin C., *The West of Alfred JacobMiller*, Norman, Oklahoma (1951), p. 67.
27 Bright, "Black Harris, Mountain Man, Teller of Tales," p. 7.
28 *Oregon Spectator*, March 4, 1847.
29 Peltier, op. cit., p. 112, quoted from a letter from Moses Harris to Thornton Grimsley, June 4, 1851.
30 Douglas, "Origins of the Population of Oregon in 1850," pp. 95–107.
31 Dale, "The Organization of the Oregon Emigrating Companies," p. 212.
32 Thomas, "George Bush."
33 Minto, "Reminiscences," pp. 212, 213.
34 Thomas, op. cit. He is quoting from a manuscript by Ezra Meeker in the Northwest Collection, University of Washington Library.
35 Blankenship, Georgiana, *Early History of Thurston County, Washington, Together with Biographies and Reminiscences of those identified with Pioneer Days*, pp. 323–4.

Chapter 2

1 Photostatic copies of this court case are in the University of Oregon Library, Special Collection.
2 *Oregon Spectator*, September 2, 1851.
3 The exclusion law passed in 1844 contained a provision requiring slaveowners to free their slaves. See appendix for text of law. See also resolutions to protect slave property presented in the legislative assembly of 1857 and 1858, and other evidence of slavery discussed in Chapter 4.
4 Minto, op. cit., p. 130.
5 Gray, *A History of Oregon, 1792–1849*, p. 255.
6 *Oregon Provisional and Territorial Papers*, Document #3515, Oregon Historical Society Manuscript Collection.
7 Ibid., Document #621.
8 *Oregon Statesman*, January 13, 1857.
9 Applegate, "Views of Oregon History," Yoncalla, Oregon (1878). Unpublished manuscript, Bancroft Library, Berkeley California.
10 *Jeffersonian Inquirer* (Jefferson City, Mo.), October 23, 1845.
11 Burnett, *Recollections and Opinions of an Old Pioneer*, p. 7.
12 Ibid., pp. 218–220.
13 Catterall, *Judicial Cases Concerning Slavery and the Negro*, pp. 333–4.
14 Thurston, *Letter of the Delegate From Oregon to the Members of the House of Representatives,* First Session, 31st Congress. Oregon Historical Society Manuscript Collection.

Chapter 3

1 Culmer, "Emigrant Missourians in Mexico and Oregon." Reprinted here is a letter from Nathaniel Ford to James A. Shirley, June 22, 1852.
2 Williams, "Political History of Oregon," pp. 5–6. For a transcript of the court case see Lockley, 'The Case of Robin Holmes vs. Nathaniel Ford," pp. 111–137.
3 c.f. discussion of "Free State Letter," pp. 50–51.
4 See page 57.
5 Jesse Applegate to Joseph Lane, November 1, 1851. MSS 51146, Oregon Historical Society Manuscript Collection. Botany Bay in Australia was a

settlement area for convicts in the 1870s.

6 Woodward, "Political Parties in Oregon," p. 126.
7 Smith became a U.S. Senator; Nesmith, U.S. Senator and later U.S. Representative; R.P. Boise, Chief Justice of the Oregon Supreme Court; Grover, U.S. Senator and Governor of Oregon. Asahel Bush held the lucrative office of State Printer and was one of the founders of a pioneer bank.
8 Davenport, "The Slavery Question in Oregon," p. 231.
9 Woodward, op. cit., pp. 141–2.
10 Platt, "22 Letters of David Logan, Pioneer Oregon Lawyer," p. 270.
11 *Oregon Statesman*, June 13, 1851.
12 *Oregon Spectator*, September 9, 1851.
13 Ibid.
14 Ibid.
15 *Oregon Statesman*, July 14, 1855.
16 *Oregon Statesman*, July 21, 1855.
17 *Weekly Oregonian*, July 12, 1856.
18 *Weekly Oregonian*, September 20, 1856.
19 Ibid.
20 *Weekly Oregonian*, November 8, 1856.
21 Ibid.
22 *Weekly Oregonian*, December 4, 1850.
23 *Oregon Statesman*, March 31, 1857.
24 *Oregon Statesman*, August 4, 1857.
25 *Oregon Statesman*, August 18, 1857.

Chapter 4

1 Defeat was by a margin of 56 percent in 1854, 52 percent in 1855, and 51 percent in 1856. The margin of approval in 1857 was 82 percent.
2 *Oregon Statesman*, July 28, 1857.
3 Berwanger, *Frontier Against Slavery*, pp. 79–80.
4 *Weekly Oregonian*, August 22, 1857.
5 Carey, Charles H., *History of the Constitution of Oregon*, p. 29.
6 Ibid., p. 362.
7 Jesse Applegate to Matthew Deady, November 15, 1868. MSS #48, Folder #138. Oregon Historical Society Manuscript Collection.
8 Carey, op. cit., p. 385.
9 Ibid., p. 27.
10 Davenport, op. cit., p. 243.
11 Ibid., p. 226.
12 Ibid., p. 247.
13 Ibid., p. 246.
14 *Oregon Argus*, October 17, 1857.
15 Davenport, op. cit., pp. 234–5.
16 Ibid.
17 *Congressional Globe*, Vol. 45. 1st Session, 35th Congress, Part II. (May 5, 1858) p. 1964
18 Ibid., p. 1967.
19 *Congressional Globe*, Vol. 46, 1st Session, 35th Congress, Part III. p. 2205.
20 *Oregon Native Son*, "Slavery in the Pacific Northwest," p. 314.

21 *Weekly Oregonian*, January 30, 1858.
22 *Journal of the Ninth Regular Session of the House of Representatives*, p. 51.
23 *Weekly Oregonian*, December 26, 1857.
24 Ibid.
25 Ibid.
26 *Weekly Oregonian*, January 30, 1858.
27 Davenport, op. cit., p. 205.
28 Ibid., p. 227.

Chapter 5

1 Hill, "The Negro in Oregon, A Survey," p. 29. Hill's thesis, the earliest work on the history of black people of Oregon, is frequently quoted and often criticized. It is, however, a most valuable source of information for the early history of the black community of Portland, as Hill interviewed many of the early residents. Although Hill said that A.E. Flowers came to Portland in 1872, Flowers himself said that he had visited the city earlier, taking a job as a waiter at the hotel Lincoln. He then left Portland, and held various jobs in The Dalles, Walla Walla, and Lewiston, before returning to Portland to settle permanently. Three facts support the theory that Flowers was describing Portland in the 1860s, and not the 1870s, as has been widely assumed. The poll tax he mentions was passed in 1862 and repealed in 1864, although it may have been collected illegally for a few more years. The People's Church was the only black church in Portland until 1869. Blacks could not vote in Oregon until 1870, but they did vote in that year and later.
2 Williams, "Political History of Oregon, 1853–1865," p. 22–3.
3 *Petition from citizens of Multnomah County in relation to Free Negroes and Kanakas*, Oregon Archives.
4 Williams, op. cit., p. 28.
5 *Oregon Statesman*, June 10, 1861.
6 Ibid.
7 *The Organic and Other General Laws of Oregon together with the National Constitution and other Public Acts and Statutes of the United States*. 1866 edition. pp. 815–17.
8 Schneider, "The Black Laws of Oregon," p. 42.
9 *The Codes and Laws of Oregon*, 1862, p. 42.
10 *Oregon Statesman*, October 3, 1864.
11 Carey, Charles H., *General History of Oregon*, p. 784.
12 *Oregon Statesman*, July 31, 1865.
13 *Oregonian*, December 16, 1865.
14 John O. Shelton, Oregon Historical Society Manuscript Collection.
15 *Oregonian*, May 25, 1866.
16 Elliot, "Dr. Robert Newell: Pioneer," p. 113.
17 *Oregonian*, March 3, 1865.
18 *Oregon Statesman*, October 2, 1865.
19 Ibid.
20 *Acts and Resolutions of the Legislative Assembly of the State of Oregon*. 1866, p. 10.
21 *Democratic Review*, March 2, 1867.
22 *Oregon Statesman*, March 12, 1866.

23 *Oregonian*, September 12, 1867.
24 *Oregonian*, October 7, 1868.
25 *Oregonian*, September 15, 1870.
26 *Journal of the Senate*, 1870, p. 654.
27 Oregon Supreme Court: Wood vs. Fitzgerald. *Oregon Reports*, Vol. 3, September, 1870, pp. 579–80.
28 *Oregon Herald*, April 8, 1870.
29 *Oregonian*, April 3, 1870.
30 *Oregonian*, September 12, 1867.
31 *Daily Record*, January 21, 1868.

Chapter 6

1 *Portland Evening Telegram*, January 11, 1893.
2 *Oregonian*, July 23, 1978.
3 "Darky Creek" is located south of Waldport, "Nigger Brown Canyon" is in Jefferson County, "Nigger Rock," renamed "Negro Rock" is in Malheur County, and "Nigger Creek Bar" is located in the Columbia River opposite St. Helens.
4 Pauline Burch, a descendant of Nathaniel Ford, tells her version of the story in a letter in the Oregon Historical Society Manuscript Collection. See Chapter 3 for a discussion of the Ford/Holmes Case.
5 Ibid.
6 Ibid. Descendants of Ford deny that any money was demanded for Mary Jane's freedom.
7 *Oregonian*, January 27, 1924.
8 *Oregon City Enterprise*, August 16, 1912.
9 Ibid. The OBHP wishes to thank Mary Ringo King for supplying information regarding John Livingston.
10 Paul F. Keady to Elizabeth McLagan, July 13, 1978. OBHP Collection.
11 op. cit., Schneider, F. ff p. 6; McArthur, *Oregon Geographic Names*, p.763; *Oregon Argus*, January 24, 1863; *Portland Observer*, February 15, 1973; Lyman, *An Illustrated History of Walla Walla County*, pp. 345–6.
12 Steeves, *Book of Remembrance*, pp. 19–21, 29–30.
13 Journals of Thomas Fletcher Royal, Jacksonville Museum, Jacksonville, Oregon. The OBHP wishes to thank Richard Engman, Archivist, for supplying information concerning black people in Jacksonville.
14 Ibid.
15 Atwood, Kay, comp., *Minorities of early Jackson County, Oregon*. Jackson Co. Intermediate Education District, 1976.
16 *Grant County News*, August 26, 1886, and February 13, 1890. The OBHP wishes to thank Laura Legler, John Day, and Janice Justice, Curator of the Herman and Eliza Oliver Historical Museum for their assistance in providing information and photographs of the Sewell family.
17 O. H.S. Vertical File, *Weekly Oregonian*, December 11, 1856, op. cit., Killian, p. 139.
18 The census figures for 1870 are confusing, given other available information on the size of the black population. The City Directory for Portland in 1870 listed 28 employed black adults, and a total black population of 137. This figure is probably low. Blacks were slighted as much as other minorities; for some

years the Chinese population is totally ignored. If the original census records themselves are examined, which is a tedious process full of pitfalls, a total black population in Oregon of less than 200 can be derived, with 90 people living in Multnomah County. Even some of these people are questionable, as people born in Hawaii are listed as black, as well as some American Indians. A further note which only adds to the confusion: in 1870 the *Oregon Herald* reported that there were 200 black males of voting age living in Portland. *Oregon Herald*, April 24, 1870.

19 0.2 percent of the total population of the city of Albina, and 0.3 percent of the population of East Portland in 1890 were black.

20 The Chinese population of Portland in 1880 was 9,515. 96 percent lived on the west side.

21 MacColl, *The Shaping of a City*, footnote, p. 3.

22 Hill, "The Negro in Oregon, A Survey," p. 38.

23 *Salem Daily Record*, January 3, 1868.

24 *Oregon Herald*, January 5, 1869.

25 *Oregonian*, April 7, 1870.

26 Op. cit., Hill, p. 40.

27 See Chapter 9.

Chapter 7

1 The *New Age*, May 10, 1902.

2 The *New Age*, November 8, 1902.

3 The *New Age*, July 16, 1904.

4 The *New Age*, April 29, 1905.

5 The *New Age*, October 13, 1906.

6 The *New Age*, May 5, 1900.

7 The *New Age*, December 27, 1902.

8 Although local library holdings of the *Advocate* do not exist prior to 1923, the Portland City Directory of 1904 lists the *Advocate* in its section on local newspapers, and in the September 1, 1923 issue, the paper announced that it was celebrating its twentieth year of publication. Some issues of the *Advocate* prior to 1923 exist in private collections which have been made available to the Oregon Black History Project.

9 The Oregon Black History Project has copies of portions of the August 2, 1919 issue. The original exists in a private collection.

10 The *New Age*, March 2, 1907.

11 The *Advocate*, December 20, 1913.

12 Longtime residents recall that a few Chinese-owned restaurants would serve black people. Some black-owned establishments were the Athenia Club (1899), Climax Cafe (1901–1906), Chile Bill's (1902), The Monogram (1902), Kentucky Kitchen (1903), Alcazar (1904), Arcadia Saloon (1904), Club Café (1904), Albina Club (1906), The Alpha (1906), Mitchell's Cafe (1919), Lunetta Soft Drink Parlor (1919), S.S. Walker's Soft Drink Parlor (1919), Barbecue Restaurant (1919), Dreamland Cafe (1924), the Hegpeth Restaurant (1910), and the Golden Rule Cafe (1929).

13 Oregon Black History Project Oral History Collection.

14 W.L. Brady (1894–1920s), Wm. Booker (1919), Crawford and Crawford (1919), Barette and Johnson (1904), Anna Hall (1906), Julia & Lewis Fuller

(1913), and Cadolia Vessell (1923).

15 Boarding houses were owned by Mrs. Hattie Smith (1903), "The Castle," (1902), "The Butler," (1903). S.S. Freeman had a butcher shop and grocery store in 1900, E.I. Jones had a fish and game market in 1902, J.B. Simmons owned a grocery store (1906), Mack Oliver owned a grocery store (1919). In 1919 three men conducted transfer and storage businesses: E.R. Richardson, V.E. Keene, Wm. Moore. J.W. Curry, an employee of the S.P. & S. line, ran a tent camp called "Sunflower Camp" in the 1920s, Perry Thompson had a catering business in 1906, and Fred D. Thomas and his wife ran a catering business from their home for many years. Two furniture dealers: E. Freeman (1919), and P.J. Summers. Duke Jackson & Sons owned an auto repair shop, and J.S. Bell had a photography studio in Portland for 20 years.

16 The founders of the company were J.C. Logan, W.L.B. Plummer, W.H. Rutherford, L.A. Goodwin, Sim Reddy, E.W. Rutherford, J.W. Payne, Howard Sproule.

17 Enterprise Hall was apparently sold soon after, as it is not listed in the City Directory for 1910.

18 The *Advocate*, September 10, 1927.

19 The *New Age*, April 12, and May 10, 1902.

20 Although the article does not specify his job, it was probably a janitorial position. He was later a janitor and then head porter at the post office. The *New Age*, December 27, 1902, October 3, 1903.

21 Flowers Family Memorabilia, Oregon Historical Society Manuscript Collection.

22 *Portland Times*, August 2, 1919.

23 Hill, E. Shelton, "The Occupational Status of the Negro Worker in the Portland Area."

24 Oregon Black History Project Oral History Collection.

25 Ibid.

26 Ibid.

27 Bethel A.M.E. Church (Larrabee and McMillen), Mount Olivet Baptist Church (East First and Schuyler), First A.M.E. Zion (417 Williams Avenue), The Independent Baptist Church (N. 10th St.), St. Phillips Mission (24th and Savier), and the Pentecostal Mission of the Church of God in Christ (28 Union Ave. N.). The Advocate, August 11, 1923.

28 The *Advocate*, July 16, 1932, Flowers Family Memorabilia (OHS Manuscript Collection), Hill, "The Negro in Oregon, A Survey."

29 New Northwest Lodge, 1883 (Odd Fellows), Enterprise Lodge of Prince Hall Masons (1883).

30 Some of the original members were Lillian Allen, Mrs. H.M. Grayson, Mrs. Waldo Bogle, Mrs. W.R. Peck, Mrs. W.H. Lewis, Edith Gray, Dolly Parries, Mrs. J.W. Payne.

31 The original officers were W.L. Brady, President; W.H. Bolds, Vice President; D.H. Lee, Recording Secretary; Rev. E.I. Swan, Corresponding Secretary; James Fullilove, Treasurer, and S.F. Collins, Chaplain.

32 The *New Age*, March 19, 1904.

33 The *New Age*, March 26, 1904.

34 The *New Age*, April 12, 1902.

35 The first officers of the NAACP were J.A. Merriman, President; Mrs. E.D. Cannady, Secretary; Mr. J.S. Bell, Treasurer; Executive Committee: Mr. E.D.

Cannady, Joseph Miller, E.G. Dickens.

36 Some membership statistics for the years between 1920 and 1940: 115 (1923), 48 (1924), 110 (1925), 121 (1926), 63 (1927), 41 (1928), 694 (1928), 357 (1931), and nearly 400 (1938). NAACP Microfilm, OBHP Collection.
37 The *Advocate*, March 22, 1930: "We wonder what the local branch of the [NAACP] is doing to check the wave of discrimination and segregation sweeping our city and state. We do not say that the association is not doing anything, but we fail to see that it is producing results along this line."
38 The *Advocate*, April 26, 1930.
39 See chapters 8 and 9.
40 The *Advocate*, November 7, 1925.
41 The *Advocate*, May 19, 1923.
42 The *Advocate*, February 28, 1925.
43 The *Advocate*, June 27, 1931.
44 Clarence Ivey to Walter White, October 27, 1933. NAACP Microfilm, OBHP Collection.
45 Ibid., E. Williams to Walter White, May 6, 1938.
46 OBHP Oral History Collection.
47 Ibid.

Chapter 8

1 Oregon Black History Project Oral History Collection.
2 The *Advocate*, August 11, 1923.
3 Oregon Black History Project Oral History Collection.
4 *Oregonian*, May 20, 1905.
5 This decision was upheld by an Oregon Supreme Court Decision in 1906. The *Oregonian*, March 6, 1906.
6 The *Advocate*, March 14, 1925.
7 The *Advocate*, December 8, 1928.
8 The *Advocate*, August 24, 1929, October 5, 1929.
9 The *Advocate*, April 18, 1922.
10 Ibid.
11 *Oregonian*, April 22, 1922.
12 Oregon Black History Project oral history collection.
13 The *New Age*, April 6, 1907.
14 The *Advocate*, July 26, 1930.
15 The *Advocate*, August 15, 1925.
16 The *Advocate*, May 26, 1923.
17 NAACP Microfilm, Oregon Black History Project.
18 The *Advocate*, March 14, 1931.
19 NAACP Microfilm, Oregon Black History Project.
20 The *Advocate*, December 29, 1923.
21 The *Advocate*, January 2, 1932.
22 The woolen mill at Oregon City was severely damaged by a fire that occurred in 1872, and circumstances surrounding the affair led to the belief that the fire was deliberately set. The mill had hired Chinese workers; those opposed to their employment formed a White Laborers Association. It was alleged that opponents to hiring Chinese were members of the K.K.K. In spite of protests and strikes the Chinese workers were retained. In November 1872

a fire was discovered at the mill. The watchman's dog had been poisoned, and the watchman reported that he had seen three men leaving the mill after he discovered a fire in three different areas of the building. When someone attempted to sound an alarm bell, they found the rope had been cut. Most of the wool and dye was saved and while the fire threatened nearby buildings, the efforts of the firefighters, lack of wind, and a drizzling rain confined the fire to the wool factory. A contemporary account speculated about the origins of the fire, saying it could have been caused by spontaneous combustion, but recognizing that prejudice against the Chinese employees was very strong and frequently expressed. Sources for this incident are the *Oregonian*, November 23, 1872, and Lomax, Alfred, "Oregon City Woolen Mill," *Oregon Historical Quarterly*, Vol. 32, pp. 256–261.

23 *Oregon Journal*, September 18, 1902.
24 *Oregonian*, September 18, 1902.
25 *Oregonian*, September 20, 1902.
26 *Oregonian*, September 21, 1902.
27 The *New Age*, September 20, 1902.
28 NAACP Microfilm, Oregon Black History Project.
29 Ibid.
30 *Oregon Voter*, August 12, 1922.
31 *Capital Journal*, October 25, 1922.
32 The *Advocate*, June 9, 1923.
33 NAACP Microfilm, Oregon Black History Project.
34 Ibid.
35 Oregon Black History Project Oral History collection. Other references that mention incidents involving Klan terrorism are: Rothwell, "The K.K.K. in the State of Oregon," p. 138, *Pacific Northwest Quarterly*, April 1962, p. 60; *Oregon Historical Quarterly*, June, 1974, footnote p. 188; *Free Land for Free Men*, p. 585.
36 The *New Age*, October 17, 1903.
37 From a manuscript written by Mrs. Garner, Oregon Black History Project Collection.
38 Crowell, "Twentieth Century Black Women in Oregon," pp. 13–15.
39 The *Advocate*, September 11, 1926.
40 Interview with black residents, Oregon Black History Project oral history collection.
41 NAACP Microfilm, OBHP collection.
42 OBHP Oral History collection.
43 *Oregon Journal*, March 6, 1919.
44 The *Advocate*, July 12, 1930.
45 NAACP Microfilm.
46 The *Advocate*, October 5, 1929.
47 Op. cit., Crowell. According to school officials, the reasons for banning black women from campus housing was that all the rooms were designed to house four women, and four black women had never applied to live in campus housing at one time.
48 OBHP Oral history collection.
49 The *New Age*, May 31, 1902.
50 The *New Age*, July 5, 1902.

51 The *New Age*, November 10, 1906.
52 The *Advocate*, November 1, 1924.
53 Hill, "The Occupational Status of the Negro Worker in the Portland Area."
54 OBHP oral history collection.
55 NAACP microfilm, OBHP collection.
56 OBHP oral history collection.

Chapter 9

1 These sections are Article 1 Sections 31, 35, and Article XV Section 8. See appendix for the text of these sections.
2 *Journal of the House*, 1891.
3 *Oregon Statesman*, January 12, 1893.
4 *Oregonian*, June 4, 1900.
5 The final tally was 19,074 in favor of repeal, 19,999 opposed.
6 The *New Age*, June 9, 1900.
7 The *New Age*, February 3, 1903.
8 Schneider, "The Black Laws of Oregon," p. 87. His source is a personal interview with Mrs. Clifford Dixon, black resident of Portland.
9 MacColl, *The Growth of A City*, p. 154.
10 Voter's Pamphlet, 1926, p. 9.
11 *Oregonian*, August 23, 1926.
12 *Oregonian*, October 17, 1926.
13 The *Advocate*, August 28, 1926.
14 The measure did, however, receive more favorable votes than any of the other amendments submitted to the voters that year.
15 The *Advocate*, November 6, 1926.
16 Article II, Section 6. The specific section this first effort sought to repeal was Article II, Section 2. It aimed to delete the word "white" from this article, and proposed to add a provision which would allow the legislature to regulate suffrage through uniform registration laws. If passed, this would have given the legislature the same power as was being exercised by southern legislatures who effectively barred most blacks from voting.
17 Op. cit., Schneider. His source is a personal interview with Henrietta Marshall, black resident of Portland.
18 Voter's Pamphlet, 1916, p. 6.
19 *Oregonian*, November 6, 1916.
20 *Oregon Voter*, December 16, 1916.
21 The *Advocate*, June 23, 1927.
22 *Oregonian*, February 2, 1893.
23 *Oregon Statesman*, February 3, 1893.
24 MacColl, *The Shaping of A City*. p. 237.
25 Lewis' motivation for introducing the bill, in his own words, was "at the request of my colored constituents." The *Oregonian* article referring to the fact that Lewis introduced many bills, called it "Lewis' bill factory." The *Oregonian*, January 9, 1917. Lewis' commitment and interest in the rights of black people was clearly indicated by his cowardly attempt to evade voting on the public accommodations bill in 1919.
26 *Oregonian*, January 11, 1917.
27 *Oregonian*, January 12, 1917.

28 It became House Bill #344.
29 The group of representatives from Multnomah County were called the Multnomah Delegation.
30 *Oregon Journal*, February 21, 1919.
31 It is difficult to find a regional pattern in the vote. The 24 favorable votes came from representatives from around the state, and many counties were divided. Even of the Multnomah Delegation eight favored the bill, while four were opposed.
32 The NAACP lobbied for a bill in every session between 1919 and 1953, often without success.
33 The Senators who introduced the bill were Allan A. Bynon, Harry L. Corbett, Joe E. Dunne, Dorothy M. Lee, and Isaac E. Staples. The *Advocate*, April 8, 1933.
34 The nine members who supported the bill were beside the five who had introduced it, Joel C. Booth, Republican from Lane and Linn counties; Henry L. Hess, Democrat from Union and Wallowa counties; William F. Woodward, Republican from Multnomah County; and Peter Zimmerman, Republican from Lincoln, Sherman, Washington and Yamhill counties.
35 *Oregon Voter*, March 18, 1933.
36 Ibid.
37 The *Advocate*, April 8, 1933.
38 *Oregonian*, January 31, 1937.
39 There was a definite regional pattern to this vote. Votes in favor were cast by Senators from Portland and the surrounding counties with one exception: one Senator from Multnomah County voted against the bill. He was also the only Democrat of eight to cast a negative vote. The other votes in favor came from Senators from northeastern and far eastern counties. The Senator from Coos and Curry counties also voted yes. Opposition to the bill came from down-state Willamette valley counties, and southern and near south and central eastern counties. The one exception to this bloc was the Senator from Benton and Polk counties who voted in favor of the bill.
40 *Oregon Voter*, March 18, 1939.
41 See appendix for text.
42 Quintard Taylor, "Blacks in the American West: An Overview."
43 The failure to pass an exclusion law was attributed not to a positive racial atmosphere, but to the fear of congressional objection, a large Oriental population, and to the existing black population which was racially mixed. Berwanger, "The 'Black Law' Question in Ante-Bellum California," p. 205.

Chapter 10
1 *Oregonian*, October 4, 1942.
2 *Oregonian*, August 18, 1946.
3 *Seattle Northwest Enterprise*, November 25, 1942.
4 "The Negro in Portland," *Portland City Club Bulletin*, 1945, p. 58.
5 *Oregonian*, April 23, 1947.
6 See Chapter 9.
7 Interview with black resident, OBHP oral history collection.
8 *Oregonian*, September 30, 1942.
9 *Oregonian*, October 4, 1942.

10 *Oregonian*, October 1, 1942.
11 *Oregonian*, October 4, 1942.
12 *Oregonian*, June 24, 1945.
13 Interview with black resident, OBHP oral history collection.
14 "Report on the Negro in Portland: A Progress Report 1945–1957," *Portland City Club Bulletin*, 1957, p. 358.
15 Jeffrey Holbrook, first vice president of the Portland Realty Board, quoted in the *Oregon Journal*, May 17, 1954.
16 Some instances of "panic selling" were noted, but even in this category all but one of the houses were sold at a profit. The study concluded that three factors had more influence on selling price than the racial nature of the neighborhood: the age, size, and type of house involved; the desirability of the neighborhood, and the degree of haste involved in completing a sale. "Non White Neighbors and Property Prices in Portland, Oregon, and Residential Attitudes toward Negroes as Neighbors," Portland, Urban League Studies, 1956.
17 The seven schools are Humboldt, Woodlawn, King, Vernon, Boise, Eliot and Sabin.
18 Op. cit., *Portland City Club Report*, 1957, p. 362. The report noted that the state had no power to investigate or initiate claims, and that no criminal penalties were attached to violations of the law.
19 Ibid., p. 365.
20 Ibid., p. 355.
21 Little and Weiss, *Blacks in Oregon, a Statistical and Historical Report*, p. 122.
22 OBHP oral history collection.

Bibliography

Oral Interviews

Kathyrn Bogle
Asa Boles
Arthur and Etoille Cox
Audrey Ellis
Therese Flowers
Rachel Green
Bessie Hale
Inglis Hegpeth
Mr. and Mrs. Julian G. Henson
Estelle Gragg
Erma Hepburn
E. Shelton Hill
James Hunter
Paul Keady
Ellen Law
James Lee
Ruby Maddox
Dick and Inez Mayberry
Mary Morton
Herman C. Plummer
Mark Parker
Alicia Reynolds
Warren Robinson
Otto Rutherford
Marie Smith
Oliver E. Smith
The Reverend L.O. Stone
James C. Strawder
Lucius Washington
Mrs. J.L. Wasson
Eddie Watson
Annie B. Williams
Maude Banks Young

Taken between 1977 and 1979. Property of the Oregon Black History Project.

Manuscripts and Letters

Applegate, Jesse. Letter to Matthew Deady, November 15, 1868, MSS #48, Folder #138, Oregon Historical Society Manuscript Collection.

___. Letter to Joseph Lane, November 1, 1851. MSS #1146, Oregon Historical Society Manuscript Collection.

___. "Views of Oregon History." Yoncalla, Oregon, 1878. Unpublished manuscript, Bancroft Library, University of California.

Burch, Pauline. "Pioneer Nathaniel Ford and the Negro Family." Albany, Oregon, 1952. MSS #707, Oregon Historical Society Manuscript Collection.

Cannady, Beatrice. Scrapbook, 1929-1936. Microfilm #160, Oregon Historical Society Manuscript Collection.

Deady, Matthew. Correspondence. MSS #48, 581, Oregon Historical Society Manuscript Collection.

Flowers, Allen Elmer. "Family Memorabilia." MSS #1049, Oregon Historical Society Manuscript Collection.

Grand Emancipation Celebration, 1869. MSS #3404, Oregon Historical Society Manuscript Collection.

Jacobs, Orange. Letter to Benjamin Dowell, October 23, 1867. MSS #209, Oregon Historical Society Manuscript Collection.

Jones, D.H. Correspondence. MSS #898, Oregon Historical Society Manuscript Collection.

Moss, Sidney W. "Pictures of Pioneer Times at Oregon City." MSS #1067, Oregon Historical Society Manuscript Collection.

Oregon Emigration Society. Articles of Agreement, circa 1839. Oregon Historical Society Manuscript Collection.

Royal, Thomas F. Journals. Jacksonville Museum, Jacksonville.

Shelton, J.V. Information on Knights of the Golden Circle. MSS #468, Oregon Historical Society Manuscript Collection.

Thurston, Samuel. "Letter of the Delegate from Oregon to the Members of the House of Representatives, First Session, 31st Congress." Oregon Historical Society Manuscript Collection.

___. Letter to Wesley Shannon, June 22, 1850. MSS #161, Oregon Historical Society Manuscript Collection.

Unpublished Works

Henderson, Archie Marie. "Introduction of the Negroes into the Pacific Northwest 1788-1842." M.A. Thesis, University of Washington, 1949.

Hill, Daniel G. "The Negro in Oregon: A Survey." M.A. Thesis, University of Oregon, 1932.

Hopkins, Oznathylee Alverdo. "Black Life in Oregon, 1899-1907: A Study of the Portland New Age." B.A. Thesis, Reed College, 1974.

Pilton, James William. "Negro Settlement in British Columbia 1858-1871." M.A. Thesis, University of British Columbia, 1951.

Poulton, Helen Jean. "The Attitude of Oregon Toward Slavery and Secession." M.A. Thesis, University of Oregon, 1946.

Rhodes, Ethel C. "Negroes in Pacific Coast History Prior to 1865." M.A. Thesis, Howard University, 1940.

Rothwell, Charles Easton. "The Ku Klux Klan in the State of Oregon." B.A. Thesis, Reed College, 1924.

Schneider, Franz M. "The Black Laws of Oregon." M.A. Thesis, University of Santa Clara, 1970.

Thomas, Paul F. "George Bush." M.A. Thesis, University of Washington, 1965.

Newspapers

Advocate, Portland
Capital Journal, Salem
Daily Record, Salem
Democratic Review, Eugene
Enterprise, Oregon City
Evening Telegram, Portland
Grant County News, Canyon City
Jeffersonian Inquirer, Jefferson City, Missouri
New Age, Portland
Northwest Enterprise, Seattle
Oregon Argus, Oregon City
Oregon Herald, Portland
Oregon Journal, Portland
Oregon Spectator, Oregon City
Oregon Statesman, Oregon City, Corvallis, Salem
Oregon Voter, Portland
Portland Observer, Portland
Portland Times, Portland
Oregonian, *Weekly Oregonian*, Portland
Times, Seattle

Public Documents, Archives, Reports

A Study of Awareness of the Oregon Fair Housing Law and a Sampling of Attitudes Toward Integrated Neighborhood Living. League of Women Voters of Portland, Oregon, 1961.

City Club of Portland. "The Negro in Portland." *Portland City Club Bulletin*, July 2, 1945, pp. 52–69.

___. "Report on the Negro in Portland: A Progress Report 1945–1957." *Portland City Club Bulletin*, April 1, 1966, pp. 111–146.

Hill, E. Shelton. *The Occupational Status of the Negro Worker in the Portland Area*. Oregon Bureau of Labor, December 7, 1950.

National Association for the Advancement of Colored People—Portland, Oregon. Official documents of the NAA CP, 1914, 1918–1955. NAACP Register, Library of Congress. 2 reels, microfilm, Oregon Black History Project.

Oregon. *Laws of a General and Local Nature Passed by the Legislative Committee and Legislative Assembly of the Territory of Oregon, 1843-1849*. Salem, Oregon: Asahel Bush, Territorial Printer, 1853.

___. *The Oregon Archives: Including the Journals, Governor's Messages, and Public Papers of Oregon, to 1849*. Salem, Oregon: Asahel Bush, Territorial Printer, 1853.

___. *The Organic and Other General Laws of Oregon Together with National Constitution and Other Public Acts and Statutes of the United States, 1845 to 1864*. Matthew P. Deady, compilator and annotator. Portland: Henry L. Pittock, State Printer, 1866.

___. Legislative Assembly. *A Code of Civil Procedure, and other general statutes of Oregon, enacted by the Legislative Assembly at the session commencing September 8, A. D. 1862*. State Printer, 1863.

___. *Acts and Resolutions of the Legislative Assembly of the state of Oregon*. 1866. Salem: W.A. McPherson, State Printer, 1866.

___. *Journals of the Proceedings of the House and Council of the Legislative Assembly of the Territory of Oregon*. Salem, Oregon: Territorial Printer, 1850-1857.

___. *Journals of the House and Senate of the Legislative Assembly of the State of Oregon*. (Sessions of 1 862, 1 864, 1865, 1866, 1868, 1870, 1872, 1891, 1893, 1895, 18 99, 1901, 1 90 3, 190 9, 1911, 1 915, 1919, 1925, 1 937, 1939.)

Salem, Oregon: State Printer.

___. Provisional and Territorial Papers. Documents #621, 3515, 8661, 9152, 9671, 11601, 10964, 1097 3, 10974, 1226. Oregon Historical Society Manuscript Collection.

___. Secretary of State. *Abstract of Votes: Constitutional Amendments and Measures*. (General Elections: 1900, 1916, 1926; Special Election, 1 927.) Salem, Oregon: Oregon State Library.

___. *Constitutional Amendments and Measures to be Submitted to the Voters of Oregon*. (General Elections: 1916, 1926; Special Election, 1 927.) Salem, Oregon: Oregon State Library.

___. "Petitions from Citizens of Multnomah County in relation to Free Negroes and Mulattoes." Item 7, Box 6. 18 62. Oregon State Archives, Salem.

___. Supreme Court. *Wood v. Fitzgerald*. Oregon Reports, Vol. 3, September 1870, pp. 568-585.

___. Territorial Government Auditor. "Assessment Rolls of Polk County, 1854." Document #1417 8, p. 9. Oregon State Archives, Salem.

___. Portland Negro Progressive Association, Inc. Documents. Folder 61-11, Item 8. Oregon State Archives, Salem.

Urban League of Portland. *Non-white Neighbors and Property Prices in Portland, Oregon; and Residential Attitudes Toward Negroes as Neighbors*. Portland, Oregon, 1956.

U.S. District Court. Oregon. Documents concerning the case of Theophilus Magruder vs. Jacob Vanderpool, 1851. University of Oregon Library, Special Collection.

Books and Periodical References

Allen, A. J. *Ten Years in Oregon*. Ithaca, New York: Mack Andrius & Company, 1848.

Anderson, Jervis. A. *Philip Randolph; a Biographical Portrait*. New York: Harcourt Brace Janovich, Inc., 1973.

Applegate, Lindsay. "Notes and Reminiscences of Laying Out and Establishing the Old Emigrant Road into Southern Oregon in the year 1846." *Oregon Historical Quarterly*, Vol. 22 #1 (March 1921), pp. 12–45.

Appleman, Roy E. *Lewis and Clark: Historic Places Associated with their Transcontinental Exploration*. Washington: U.S. National Park Service, 1975.

Atwood, Kay. *Minorities of Early Jackson County, Oregon*. Jackson County Intermediate Education District, 1976.

Ayer, John Edwin, "George Bush, the Voyageur," *Washington Historical Quarterly*, Vol. 7 #1 (January 1915), pp. 40–45.

Bakeless, John. *Lewis and Clark: Partners in Discovery.* New York: William Morrow & Co., 1947. Bancroft, Hubert Howe. History of Oregon, 1834-1888. San Francisco: The History Co. 1886-88.

___. *History of the Northwest Coast.* San Francisco: The History Co. 1886–88.

Belknap, George N. Oregon Imprints. Eugene: University of Oregon, 1968.

Bergquist, James M. "The Oregon Donation Act and National Land Policy," *Oregon Historical Quarterly,* Vol. 58 1 (March 1957), pp. 17–35.

Berwanger, Eugene H. *Frontier Against Slavery.* Urbana: University of Illinois Press, 1967.

___ . "The 'Black Law' Question in Ante-Bellum California." *Journal of the West,* Vol. 6 (April 1967) pp. 205–220.

Blankenship, Georgiana, ed. *Early History of Thurston County, Washington.* Olympia, Washington, 1914.

Bright, Verne. "Black Harris, Mountain Men, Teller of Tales." *Oregon Historical Quarterly,* Vol. 52 #1 (March 1951), pp. 3–20.

Burnett, Peter. "Recollections of an Old Pioneer." *Oregon Historical Quarterly,* Vol. 5 #1 (March 1904).

___. *Recollections and Opinions of an Old Pioneer.* New York: D. Appleton & Co., 1880. Reprint. New York: Da Capo Press, 1969.

Camp, Charles ed. *James Clyman, Frontiersman.* Portland, Oregon: Champoeg Press, 1960.

Carey, Charles H. *General History of Oregon.* Portland, Oregon: Binford and Mort, 1971.

___. The Oregon Constitution and Proceedings and Debates of the Constitutional Convention of 1857. Salem, Oregon: State Printing Office, 1926.

Catterall, Helen H. *Judicial Cases Concerning Slavery and the Negro.* New York: Octagon Books, 1968.

Chittenden, Hiram M. *The American Fur Trade of the Far West.* New York: The Press of the Pioneers, 1935.

Clark, Robert C. "The Chief Factors of the Columbia Department (1821–1846)." *Pacific Northwest Quarterly,* Vol. 28 #4 October 1937.

___ . "The Last Step in the Formation of a Provisional Government for Oregon in 1845." Oregon Historical Quarterly, Vol. 161 December 1915, pp. 313–329.

Corning, Howard Mc Kinley. *Dictionary of Oregon History.* Portland: Binford & Mort publishers, 1956.

Crowell, Evelyn. "Twentieth Century Black Women in Oregon." Northwest Journal of African and Black American Studies, Vol. 1 1, (1973), pp. 13-15. Culmer, Frederic A., ed. "Emigrant Missourians in Mexico and Oregon."*Missouri Historical Review,* Vol. 25 (1931), p. 287.

Curry, George B. "Address Before the Oregon Pioneer Association." *Transactions of the Oregon Pioneer Association,* 1887.

Dale, Harrison C. "The Organization of the Oregon Emigrating Companies." *Oregon Historical Quarterly,* Vol. 16 #3 (Sept. 1915), pp. 205–227.

Davenport, T.W. "Slavery Question in Oregon." *Oregon Historical Quarterly,* Vol. 8 #3 (Sept. 1908), pp. 189–253.

Davis Lenwood G. "Sources for History of Blacks in Washington State." *Western Journal of Black Studies,* Vol. 2 #1 (March 1978), pp. 60-64.

Douglas, Jesse S. "Origins of the Population of Oregon in 1850." *Pacific Northwest Quarterly,* Vol. 41 2 (April 1950), pp. 95–107.

Drotning, Philip, *A Guide to Negro History*. Garden City, New York: Doubleday, 1968.

Drury, Clifford. *Marcus and Narcissa Whitman and the Opening of Old Oregon*. Glendale, Calif: A.H. Clark Co. 1973.

Elliot, T.C. "The Coming of the White Woman." *Oregon Historical Quarterly*, Vol. 38 #1 (March 1937), p. 49.

___. "Doctor' Robert Newell: Pioneer." *Oregon Historical Quarterly*, Vol. 9 #2 (June 1908), p. 113.

Ellison, Joseph. "Designs for a Pacific Republic, 1843-62." *Oregon Historical Quarterly*, Vol. 31 #4 (Dec. 1930), p. 342.

"Emigration to Oregon." *Iowa Journal of History and Politics*, Vol. 10 #3 (July 1912), pp. 418–424.

Fenton, William D. "Political History of Oregon from 1865–1876." *Oregon Historical Quarterly*, Vol. 2 #4 (Dec. 1901), pp. 321–365.

Fremont, John Charles. *Report of the Exploring Expedition to the Rocky Mountains in the year 1842, and to Oregon and north California in the years 1843-'44*. Washington: Blair and Rives, printers, 1845.

Geer, Theodore T. *Fifty Years in Oregon; experiences, observations and commentaries upon men, measures, and customs in pioneer days and later times*. New York: The Neal Publishing Co., 1912.

Gray, W. H. *A History of Oregon, 1792-1849*. Portland: Hams & Holman, pub., 1870.

Haines, Francis D. Jr. *Jacksonville, Biography of a Gold Camp*. Gandee Printing Center, 1967.

Hayes, Marjorie M. *The Land That Kept its Promise*. Newport, Oregon: Lincoln County Historical Society, 1976.

Hendrickson, James E. *Joe Lane of Oregon, Machine Politics and the Sectional Crisis, 1849-1861*. New Haven and London: Yale University Press, 1967.

Himes, George H. "Constitutional Convention of Oregon." *Oregon Historical Quarterly*, Vol. 15 #4 (Dec. 1914), pp. 217–18.

Himes, George H. "Diary of Samuel Royal Thurston." *Oregon Historical Quarterly*, Vol. 15 #1 (March 1914), p. 179.

Holman, Frederick V. "A Brief History of the Oregon Provisional Government and what caused its formation." *Oregon Historical Quarterly*, Vol. 13 #2 (June 1912), pp. 133–135.

Holmes, Kenneth L. "James Douglas." in Hafen, LeRoy R. *The Mountain Men and the Fur Trade of the Far West*. Vol. 9. Glendale, California: A.H. Clark Co., 1965–72.

Horner, John B. *Days and Deeds in the Oregon Country*. Portland, Oregon: The J.K. Gill Co., 1928.

Hosmer, James K. *Gass's Journal of the Lewis and Clark Expedition*. Chicago: A. C. McClurg and Company, 1904.

Howay, Frederic W., ed. *Voyages of the "Columbia" to the Northwest Coast, 1787–1790*. Massachusetts Historical Society, 1941.

Hull, Dorothy. "The Movement in Oregon For the Establishment of a Pacific Coast Republic." *Oregon Historical Quarterly*, Vol. 17 #3 (Sept. 1916), pp. 177–200.

Irving, Washington. *Astoria, or Anecdotes of an Enterprise Beyond the Rocky Mountains*. Philadelphia, 1836.

Jackson, Donald, ed. *Letters of the Lewis and Clark Expedition with related documents 1783-1854*. Urbana: University of Illinois Press, 1962.

Johannsen, Robert W., ed. "A Breckinridge Democrat on the Secession Crisis: Letters of Isaac I. Stevens, 1860–61." *Oregon Historical Quarterly*, Vol. 55 #4 (Dec. 1954), pp. 283-309.

___. *Frontier Politics and the Sectional Conflict: The Pacific Northwest on the Eve of the Civil War.* Seattle: University of Washington, 1955.

___. "The Kansas-Nebraska Act and the Pacific Northwest Frontier." *Pacific Historical Quarterly*, Vol. 22 (1953), pp. 129–141.

___. "Spectators of Disunion: The Pacific Northwest and the Civil War." *Pacific Northwest Quarterly*, Vol. 44 (1953).

Johansen, Dorothy O. "A Tentative Appraisal of Territorial Government in Oregon." *Pacific Historical Review*, Vol. 18 (1949), pp. 485-499.

Kelley, Hall Jackson. *A General Circular to all Persons of Good Character who wish to emigrate to the Oregon Territory.* Charleston: Wilham Wheildon, 1831.

Kilian, Crawford. *Go Do Some Great Thing: The Black Pioneers of British Columbia.* Vancouver B.C.: Douglas & McIntyre, Ltd. 1978.

Lee, Daniel, and Frost, J.H. *Ten Years in Oregon.* New York: Arno Press, 1973. Reprint of 1844 edition.

Little, William A. and Weiss, James E., ed. *Blacks in Oregon a statistical and historical report.* Portland: The Black Studies Center and the Center for Population Research and Census, Portland State University, 1978.

Lockley, Fred. "The Case of Robin Holmes vs. Nathaniel Ford." *Oregon Historical Quarterly*, Vol. 23 #2 (June 1922), pp. 111-137.

___. 'The McNemees and Tetherows with the Migration of 1845." *Oregon Historical Quarterly*, Vol. 25 #4 (Dec. 1924), p. 356.

___. "Some Documentary Records of Slavery in Oregon." *Oregon Historical Quarterly*, Vol. 17 #2 (June 1916), pp. 107-115.

"Louis Labonte's Recollections of Men." *Oregon Historical Quarterly*, Vol. 4 #3 (Sept. 1903), p. 265.

Lyman, Horace S. *History of Oregon.* New York: The North Pacific Publishing Society, 1903.

Lyman, William Denison. *An Illustrated History of Walla Walla County.* San Francisco: W. H. Lever, 1901.

Lynch, Vera Martin. *Free Land for Free Men: A Story of Clackamas County.* Portland: Artline Printing, 1973.

McArthur, Lewis A. *Oregon Geographic Names.* 4th Edition. Portland: Oregon Historical Society, 1974.

MacColl, E. Kimbark. *The Growth of a City. Power and Politics in Portland, Oregon 1915–1950.* Portland: The Georgian Press Company, 1979.

___. *The Shaping of a City. Business and Politics in Portland, Oregon, 1885-1915.* Portland: The Georgian Press Company, 1976.

Minto, John. "Antecedents of the Oregon Pioneers and the Light These Throw on Their Motives." *Oregon Historical Quarterly*, Vol. 5 #1 (March 1904), p. 45.

___. "Reminiscences." *Oregon Historical Quarterly*, Vol. 2 #3 (Sept. 1901), p. 212–13.

___. "What I know of Dr. McLoughlin and how I know it." *Oregon Historical Quarterly*, Vol. 11 #2 (June 1910), pp. 194, 197.

Murray, Pauli, ed. *States' laws on race and color and appendices containing international documents, federal laws and regulations, local ordinances and charts.* Cincinnati: Women's Division of Christian Service, Board of Missions and church extension, Methodist Church, 1950.

"Negro Pioneers; their Page in Oregon History." *Oregon Native Son*. Vol. 1 (1900), pp. 432–4.

Oswald, Delmont R. "James P. Beckwourth." in Hafen, LeRoy R., ed. *The Mountain Men and the Fur Trade of the Far West*. Glendale, California: A.H. Clark Co., 1965–72.

Peltier, Jerome. "Moses 'Black' Harris." in Hafen, LeRoy R., ed. *The Mountain Men and the Fur Trade of the Far West*. Glendale, California: A.H. Clark Co., 1965–72.

Peterson, Emil R. and Powers, Alfred. *A Century of Coos and Curry*. Coquille Oregon: Curry Pioneer and Historical Association, 1952.

Pioneer Ladies Club of Pendleton, comp. *Reminiscences of Oregon Pioneers*. Eastern Oregon Publishing Co., 1937.

Platt, Henry, ed. "22 letters of David Logan, Pioneer Oregon Lawyer." *Oregon Historical Quarterly*, Vol. 44 #3 (Sept. 1943).

Platt, Robert Treat. "Oregon and its Share in the Civil War." *Oregon Historical Quarterly*, vol. 4 #2 (June 1903), pp. 89–109.

Porter, Kenneth W. "Negroes and the Fur Trade." *Minnesota History: A Quarterly Magazine*, Saint Paul: The Minnesota History Society, Vol. 15#1 (March 1934), pp. 421–433.

___. "Roll of Overland Astorians, 1810–12." *Oregon Historical Quarterly*, Vol. 34 #2 (June 1933), pp. 107–8.

Potter, David M. *The Impending Crisis, 1848–1861*. New York: Harper & Row, 1976.

Powell, Fred Wilbur. "Hall Jackson Kelley." *Oregon Historical Quarterly*, Vol. 18 #2 (June 1917), p. 128.

Powers, Alfred and Finke, Mary-Jane. "Survey of First Half-Century of Oregon Hotels." *Oregon Historical Quarterly*, Vol. 43 #3 (Sept. 1942), p. 270.

Reynolds, Charles. "Portland Public Schools 1845-1871. " *Oregon Historical Quarterly*, Vol. 33 #4 (Dec. 1932), pp. 344-5.

Robinson, James R. 'The Genesis of Political Authority in Oregon." *Oregon Historical Quarterly*, Vol. 1 #1 (March 1900), p. 9, 48–59.

___. "Recollections of Alanson Hinman." *Oregon Historical Quarterly*, Vol. 2 #3 (Sept. 1901), p. 268.

Rockwood, Ruth E., ed. "Letters of Charles Stevens. " *Oregon Historical Quarterly*, Vol. 38 #2 (June 1937), pp. 183–185.

Rucker, Maude Applegate. *The Oregon Trail and Some of its Blazers*. New York: Walter Neal, 1930.

Sage, W.N. "James Douglas on the Columbia, 1830–1849." *Oregon Historical Quarterly*, Vol. 27 #4 (Dec. 1926), pp. 365–380.

Savage, W. Sherman. "The Negro in the Western Movement." *Journal of American History*, Vol. 25 (1940), p. 534–5.

___ *Blacks in the West*. Connecticut: Greenwood Press, 1976.

Shippee, Lester Burrell. "The Federal Relations of Oregon VI: Organization of Oregon as a Territory." *Oregon Historical Quarterly*, Vol. 20 #2 (June 1919), p. 275.

Simms, Henry H. "The Controversy Over the Admission of the State of Oregon." *Mississippi Valley Historical Review*, Vol. 32, pp. 355–374.

"Slavery in the Pacific Northwest." *Oregon Native Son*, Vol. 1 (Nov. 1900), p. 314.

Smith, Helen Krebs. *The Presumptuous Dreamers.* Lake Oswego: Smith, Smith and Smith, 1974.

Smith, Herndon, comp. *Centralia: The First Fifty Years 1845–1900.* Centralia Washington: Daily Chronicle and F.H. Cole Printing Co. 1942.

Smith, Willette Moore. *Oregon Pioneers of 1852 & 1853, the Snodgrass, Deckard & Moore Families.* Willette Moore Smith: 1970.

Steeves, Sarah Hunt. *Book of Remembrance of Marion County Oregon Pioneers, 1840-1860.* Salem: Berncliff Printers, 1927.

Taylor, Quintard. " Blacks in the American West: An Overview." *Western Journal of Black Studies,* Vol. 1 #1 (March 1977), pp. 4–10.

___. "Migration of Blacks and Resulting Discriminatory Practices in Washington State between 1940 and 1950." *Western Journal of Black Studies,* Vol. 2 #1 (March 1978), pp. 65–71.

Teiser, Sidney. "George H. Williams." *Oregon Historical Quarterly,* Vol. 47 #3 (Sept. 1948), pp. 255–280.

___. "The Second Chief Justice of Oregon Territory: Thomas Nelson." *Oregon Historical Quarterly,* Vol. 48 #3 (Sept. 1947), pp . 214–224.

Thornton, J. Quinn. *Oregon and California in 1848.* New York: Harper and Brothers, 1864.

Thwaites, Reuben Gold. *Original Journals of the Lewis and Clark Expedition, 1804–1806.* New York: Dodd, Mead & Company, 1904—5.

Turnbull, George S. *History of Oregon Newspapers.* Portland, Oregon: Binford & Mort, 1939.

Victor, Francis F. "Hall Kelley." *Oregon Historical Quarterly,* Vol. 2 4 (Dec. 1901), p. 387.

Williams, George H. "Political History of Oregon from 1853–1865." *Oregon Historical Quarterly,* Vol. 2 #1 (March 1901), pp. 1–35.

Wilson, Elinor. *Jim Beckwourth: Black Mountain Man and War Chief of the Crows.* University of Oklahoma Press, 1972.

Winther, Oscar Osburn. *The Old Oregon Country.* University of Nebraska Press, 1950.

Work, Monroe N. "A Negro Pioneer in the West." *Journal of Negro History,* Vol. 8 #19.

Woodward, W. C. "Political Parties in Oregon." *Oregon Historical Quarterly,* Vol. 12 #2 (June 1911).

The Rise and Early History of Political Parties in Oregon 1843–1868. Portland: J.K. Gill Co., 1913.

Further Reading for the Second Edition

Anderson, Martha. *Black Pioneers of the Northwest, 1800–1918*. Portland, Oregon: self-published, 1980.

Betts, Robert B. *In Search of York: The Slave Who Went to the Pacific with Lewis and Clark.* Boulder: University Press of Colorado, Lewis and Clark Trail Heritage Foundation, 2000.

Coleman, Kenneth R. *Dangerous Subjects: James Saules and the Rise of Black Exclusion in Oregon.* Corvallis: Oregon State University Press, 2017.

Darby, Melissa. *Thunder Go North.* Salt Lake City: University of Utah Press, 2019.

Geier, Max G. *The Color of Night: Race, Railroaders, and Murder in the Wartime West.* Corvallis: Oregon State University Press, 2015.

Hegne, Barbara. *Saga of the Mask Plantation North Carolina: Slaves Journey to Oregon.* Self-published, 2014.

___. *Settling the Rogue Valley: The Tough Times, The Forgotten People.* Self-published, 1995.

Katz, William Loren. *The Black West.* New York, New York: Doubleday Inc., 1971.

Mangun, Kimberly. A *Force for Change: Beatrice Morrow Cannady and the Struggle for Civil Rights in Oregon, 1912–1936.* Corvallis: Oregon State University Press, 2010.

Marsh, Pearl Alice. *But Not Jim Crow: Family Memories of African American Loggers of Maxville, Oregon.* Oregon: African American Loggers Project, 2019.

Nokes, R. Gregory. *Breaking Chains: Slavery on Trial in the Oregon Territory.* Corvallis: Oregon State University Press, 2013.

___. *The Troubled Life of Peter Burnett: Oregon Pioneer and First Governor of California.* Corvallis: Oregon State University Press, 2018.

Oregon Black Pioneers. *Perseverance: A History of African Americans in Oregon's Marion and Polk Counties.* Self-published, 2011.

Oregon Black Pioneers and Moreland, Kimberly Stowers. *Images of America: African Americans of Portland.* Charleston, South Carolina: Arcadia Publishing, 2013.

Taylor, Quintard. *In Search of the Racial Frontier.* New York: W.W. Norton & Co., 1998.

Index